FREEDOM BY DESIGN

THE ESTABLISHED BUSINESS OWNER'S GUIDE TO GROW, MAKE AN IMPACT, AND FIND THE JOY AGAIN

MICHAEL G. WALSH

WALSH BUSINESS GROWTH INSTITUTE

Paperback ISBN: 978-0-9953330-2-4
Ebook ISBN: 978-0-9953330-4-8

Published by:
Walsh Business Growth Institute
Vancouver, BC, Canada

Contact:
info@walshbusinessgrowth.com
www.walshbusinessgrowth.com

This book is dedicated to Grace Francescato.
My world is so much better with you in it.
Thank you!!

CONTENTS

FOREWORD

KIM FOLSOM, FOUNDER, CHAIRPERSON & CEO, FOUNDERS FIRST CAPITAL PARTNERS

I was fortunate to meet Michael Walsh in 2016, shortly after he published his second book, *Thinking Big is Not Enough*. What stood out to me immediately was his ability to translate decades of experience advising growing companies into practical, actionable frameworks that business owners could use to strengthen their organizations.

We collaborated to co-develop a three-month bootcamp accelerator program designed specifically to help companies craft and implement growth plans tailored to their needs—plans that positioned them to secure funding from our organization.

At the time, most business growth programs were focused on tech startups, pharmaceutical firms, or manufacturing companies. Yet, service-based businesses make up more than 80% of all companies in the U.S., and there were few structured resources to help them scale beyond the low seven-figure level. This gap inspired our collaboration, and Michael's expertise helped us build a program that has since supported over 1,200 businesses.

The practicality of his input was clear. Participating companies have grown by 71% within two years of completing the program and collectively raised over $200 million in funding through our platform and network of funding partners.

In Freedom by Design, Michael distills the same fundamental knowledge and skills that have empowered so many of our program participants—but he goes even further.

You will read about the underlying issues facing established and growing service-based businesses today. Business dynamics have been changing, and they have permanently shifted the economic landscape we all face.

Michael sets the stage for business owners to understand the foundational role of people in teams in dealing with these evolving issues, emphasizing the strategies for hiring, talent development, leadership growth, and delegation that are essential for scaling a services business successfully in the 21st century.

He introduces a structured approach to navigating the inevitable challenges of business growth, helping owners anticipate when and how to make key adjustments. What makes this book so impactful is its blend of real-life examples, proven strategies, and a clear framework for implementation.

Michael's ability to break down complex concepts into practical, easy-to-apply steps ensures that *Freedom by Design* will serve as a trusted guide, not just for setting business growth plans but for navigating the evolving needs of a company over time.

As a service-based business owner myself, I appreciate that this book provides a roadmap tailored to people-powered organizations—an intentional method for expanding to mid-market and beyond. *The Freedom Framework* introduced in this book is particularly valuable, offering business owners a clear perspective on how their role and strategies can evolve at different stages of growth.

I envision Freedom by Design becoming a well-used resource, revisited frequently by business owners as they refine their growth plans and guide their people forward. It is more than just a book; it is a playbook for long-term success.

Kim Folsom
Founder, Chairperson & CEO
Founders First Capital Partners

INTRODUCTION

A SPECIAL NIGHT

It was November 6. The ballroom was electric.

More than five hundred industry professionals from around the world descended on the Marriott Hotel in London's Mayfair District for this gala affair. This was the Creative and Marketing Agencies' awards night, Europe's industry event of the year.

Old friends and new acquaintances connected. Animated dinner conversations centered on who the winners might be this night. After all, this was the most elite of the industry's international competitions. More than 150 participating companies from around the globe had submitted their best, and the crowd was buzzing with anticipation. Who would be victorious in their respective categories? And who would win it all?

Sitting with her core team as the master of ceremonies warmed up the guests for the post-dinner ceremony, Maria contemplated the journey she had experienced so far.

Was it really only four years ago that her little company, with seven staff members, was earning four hundred thousand pounds[1]

1. £400,000 was $600,000 USD at the time.

per year? "The little engine that could," she had liked to call herself. My, how time flew by!

She sat among all these major players in the industry. Her firm had been nominated for Creative Agency of the Year. She never in her wildest dreams considered this as a possibility. What an adventure!

Her only dream had been to compete with the "big boys." Though she doubted it was possible, she had often yearned to build her company to one million pounds in revenue per year. If she ever got that far, she'd know she had "arrived." However, such foolish thoughts felt completely unrealistic even two years ago.

Now, with the year coming to a close, she had quintupled her company's revenue of four years earlier, effectively doubling her one-million-pound dream target. More importantly, she had finally been invited to the party with the biggest players in her industry.

An hour and a half later, her satisfaction was complete when her company name was called. She won!

This business she had been growing was so much fun! She was on top of the world.

Little did she know, this was only the start of what quickly turned into a stress-filled descent into business hell.

Three Months Later

Maria couldn't figure it out.

It had only been a few months since her company had been named Creative Agency of the Year. She felt blessed to win such a prestigious international award. After that night, the phone quickly started ringing with companies all over the world wanting to hire her firm for their projects.

Yet despite the increased interest, her sales were plummeting. Her salespeople were overworked, struggling to keep up with the increased demand for proposals. Even still, very few of the projects were closing. She had never experienced this before. And here she was, at 10:30 p.m. on a Saturday night, reviewing her team's sales pipeline, still unable to locate the problem.

This was the most stress she had been under since starting the business. What was going on?

Six Months After That

Fortunately, Maria was able to make the needed corrections in the Spring to start winning business again.

Whew!

Then a previous client reached out. They had recently merged with one of their industry partners and wanted Maria's firm to take over all of their open projects. Overnight, they went from fighting to get work to overwhelmed with the sudden increases in volume.

This kicked off a much bigger problem. Most of her production staff of thirty-five people were working sixty-hour weeks to keep up with the new business that was flowing in. They needed fifteen more people across three departments just to keep up. However, they couldn't find the right people for their teams of graphics designers, developers, and project coordinators. All three departments were full of people on the edge of burnout.

She thought she was under stress when her sales had dried up in the new year. This was worse… much worse!

Another Year and a Half Passed

The numbers for the business had continued to explode. The company eventually got past their staffing shortage, squeaking by without too much carnage. However, the chronic stress and anxiety had taken a toll on Maria's body, creating the beginnings of an ulcer.

Now, with revenue exceeding five million pounds per year, she was at a loss. Somehow, even with the growth, her profit had tanked. Money was leaking out of the company, but she couldn't find the source.

Quality had started to slip as well. The team leads in the various departments were stretched too thin, and their respective staff members were grumbling. Their reputation as a high engagement company was slipping in the marketplace.

The company had swelled to a staff of eighty to cover the workload and internal processes. Now the problem wasn't finding people. It was dealing with them. Departments were fraught with drama, high turnover, and management struggles.

For Maria, it was a constant roller coaster between low-level anxiety and nighttime sweats. She couldn't remember the last time she'd slept through the night.

She had started the business to get free from her job at the time, and the corporate life that came with it. She wanted to spend her days working on things that lit her up and have time set aside for travel with her family. She thought the company growing would allow her to step away more and more from the day to day, but instead, it had built a prison around her.

What happened?

Challenges with Business Growth

The problems confronting Maria are just a few of the many issues business owners face as they grow.

They are more common than you would think. People rarely talk about this to others in their industry. That might leave the door open to unpleasant attacks by "friendly" competitors in the market or risk the embarrassment of being the owner of a struggling company.

Frequently, business owners experience anything from low-level anxiety to periodic bouts of issue-driven panic. In other cases, they are resigned to the fact that this is the way it is. The owners are worn down. Often, they just want to sell the business and get out.

Other times, they would love to rekindle the positive energy they once experienced when the business was smaller. They just don't know if it is still possible.

Even with exciting possibilities, an unending road of hurdles seems to stand between them and the freedom they desire.

Looking for Help

At different times through a journey of business growth, business owners start looking for outside perspectives to overcome the challenges they face. While they may peruse the internet, in all but the smallest cases, they quickly move past this resource except for reference material, given the millions of proposed solutions and alternatives available.

How do you tell what's real versus what's a scam or well-intended quasi-amateurs peddling their wares?

Instead, they start reading more business books, going to industry-sponsored workshops and seminars, and talking with colleagues they trust. Their hope is to glean some nuggets that will help them to find the insights or assistance they need to move their situation forward.

Yet, even if you look at the one example from Maria, many problems seem to be specific to her situation. These problems seem impossible to solve by the vague or broad advice you so often find.

Despite the differences in issues business owners experience, as well as variance in size and scope of their growing enterprises, they are all impacted by one core, underlying issue.

That is their people.

This Book

My last book, *Thinking Big Is Not Enough*, was based on part of a journey taken by one business owner, Louise Pasterfield, to grow her e-learning company.

While Louise's situation resonated with many business owners who shared their perspectives with me, I have taken a different path with this book.

Over the past thirty years I have focused on in-depth assistance with growth strategies and implementation plans of hundreds of business owners and their companies, varying from under one million dollars to over fifty million in revenue. People just like you. Mostly I have been helping these people grow their companies in support of their goals for themselves and their families, for the company's teams, clients and customers, and in the communities in which the businesses have been operating.

The book you are reading is a departure from my previous written work. It is more about some of the specific trends I have witnessed over the past three decades, shared by the diverse mix of clients I have had the privilege to work with over that time. These trends lead to surprising implications for business owners and leaders in today's business environment.

Instead of sticking to one owner's journey, you will notice a variety of different business situations and examples. While most of the names and details within the various scenarios have been adjusted to preserve client privacy, all examples are real.

Business owners of varying sizes of organizations and in different countries have shared similarities in their journeys, despite a large variety of products and services, industries, customer bases, and even geographic and cultural differences.

I have certainly had my own eyes opened to these trends and their implications. Yet many are hidden from view.

If you are like the many business owners I have worked with, you share a drive to make things better. Further, you share a deep-seated desire to gain more freedom in your business and in your life.

One other thing you share is the need to deal with obstacles that get in the way.

The purpose of this book is to dispel the misunderstandings and hidden nuances about operating and growing an established business. My goal is to support you to deal with the underlying issues that threaten to impede or derail your attempts to grow the business you want.

This will support you in achieving your goals for increased joy, satisfaction, and, yes, even freedom in a business that is growing and thriving.

In this book, I will cover three things:

1. **Hidden Issues**. These are the aspects of your company that are impeding growth and, ultimately, keeping you chasing your tail in never-ending to-dos and problems.
2. **The Challenge**. The single issue that, when identified, understood, and addressed, will turn everything around.
3. **The Framework**. The exact methodology you as the business owner can implement to grow, make an impact, and to finally access the freedom you crave.

By the end of this book, you will be equipped with the perspectives and the tools to turn your company into the conduit for freedom within your business, from your business, and as a result of your business.

After all, isn't that what you are here for?

When all is said and done, we want a business that gives us freedom above all else.

1

FREEDOM... THE ELUSIVE GOAL

I don't know all your goals, but I do know one big one—freedom.

1. Freedom of time
2. Freedom of money
3. Freedom of self-expression
4. Freedom to make the impact you desire
5. Freedom to leave your mark on the world
6. Freedom to take care of the things that are important to you

THESE MAY BE SUMMARIZED INTO THREE CORE FREEDOMS:

1. Freedom ***in*** your business, to focus on things that bring you joy, satisfaction, and a sense of accomplishment and growth,
2. Freedom ***from*** your business, so you are not constantly tied to it, and
3. Freedom ***because of*** your business, to deal with your other goals and commitments in life.

If you can identify what constitutes freedom for you in these three areas, it becomes easier to identify the aspects of your company that rob you of that feeling. Only if you know the obstacles you must overcome can you conquer them and achieve the levels of freedom you desire in each area.

1. Freedom *in* Your Business

Some things in your business you love to do. Other things you loathe doing. The rest is just "meh."

Love ⟷ **"Meh"** ⟷ **Loath**

Figure 1.1

Whether you are solving problems, issues, and puzzles that challenge your intellect, tapping opportunities that excite you, or contributing to others in meaningful ways, some things will always give you far more energy than they take from you. Do you have the freedom to participate in these activities that give you energy? Or are you stuck handling the problems that drain you?

Some problems may keep you up at night, worried about the consequences of things turning out worse than you can afford. These stress-filled times drain away your energy and can leave you feeling stuck.

In an expertise-driven business, your growth in your specialty may have been one major area of focus and energy through your career. Many specialists gain lots of energy there. Those skills have likely helped you get to the point you are at now in your business journey. Not only that, but you may well enjoy using those skills you have developed.

Freedom ***in*** your business is having the latitude to focus your efforts on those accountabilities where you can bring your best, that have the highest strategic significance, and that you find rewarding. Have you designed your business to allow for this to occur during at least part of each day?

What are these activities? By listing them, you will gain increased access to shift the focus of your efforts in their direction.

Have you developed your business teams based upon complementary strengths, allowing each person to bring their best in ways that maximize their contribution and generate stronger results?

This is a design issue. Without active focus, it won't happen. Your freedom within your own walls is at stake.

2. Freedom *from* Your Business

Do you take enough time off?

Are you able to escape the business long enough to enjoy your family, your friends, and the activities that feed and nurture you? That could be a great meal, a concert, a sporting event, or your child's recital at school. One of the goals of business owners is to enjoy the growth of their family, their spouse or significant other, their immediate relatives, and their pets. However, this can seem like a stretch when any time away from the business feels like it would have devastating consequences.

And what about vacations? Are you able to step away from your business for a week… two… or even more with the confidence that you will come back to find it better off than you left it? Or does even the idea of a long weekend away stress you out to the point that it's not worth it?

In the early days, you may have become a servant to your business. At that time, this approach of constant care and attention may have been appropriate. If you didn't do it, you had nobody there to get it (whatever the "it" was) done. Have you been able to structure your company as you grow, to move past these habits of survival? Or are you still there?

Like freedom *in* the business, generating freedom *from* the business is a design issue, requiring time, effort, and your best focus. It rarely happens by itself—approximately 0 percent of the time.

Chronic fatigue comes from a lack of mastery to overcome the challenges that steal your freedom in this area.

3. Freedom *because of* Your Business

Then there is the pay-off. This could be financial, or it might be the impact in the world you seek to make. I have seen parents use their business to grow the character of their adult children. I regularly get to witness meaningful contributions, both financial and in measurable improvements in people's lives that result directly from intentional business activities.

Growing your asset base plays well in this area. So does a conscious focus on recipients of the services you provide.

Many owners I have supported had a clear focus to move their industry forward by improving the skills and careers of their people.

Of course, these efforts usually have a holistic effect, positively impacting providers as well as recipients of such contributions. That's what makes them so much fun to achieve.

Freedom or Money?

Many people who don't own a company think business owners are all about money. You and I know you're not all about the money. You want freedom. It's just that freedom can cost a lot of money. That's why money is a cornerstone of your business at every stage of growth.

Whether you have just recently reached the initial milestone of one million dollars per year in revenue, or if you are at a revenue level of two million, five million, ten million, twenty million, somewhere in between, or well beyond those annual revenue milestones, the money gets to be an active part of the picture, but not the end goal in itself.

If the true riches lie outside the cash, why is it such a high focus in business?

Without stability of your money, you don't gain sustainability of the impact of your efforts. And with no sustainability you can have no lasting freedom.

I have yet to interact with a company—whether it be one with five to ten people or an organization with a staff of two hundred or more—where some measure of freedom wasn't behind the goals and objectives of the owners.

Of course, freedom within your company will show up differently, depending on your current size, your goals in each area, and what you want to do with that freedom—its purpose and direction.

If freedom is such a high value for all business owners, why doesn't everyone just build their companies to attain these levels?

What stops us from achieving the freedoms we all seek?

Blockers to Freedom

As I worked with company owners in different countries throughout the world to grow their businesses—whether breaking through revenue thresholds of two million, five million, ten million or more—I started to notice specific similarities emerge with different clients. These were not the typical issues you would expect as a company grows: sales and marketing, production, money, people, or larger strategy and leadership challenges that owners invariably faced.

These issues were different. They were below the surface and not necessarily tied to any one thing. They seemed to show up around each of the major milestones of business growth and kept owners stuck in their business no matter what they tried to do to fix them.

I now refer to these critical points in business as ***Danger Zones***.

2

THE FIRST TWO DANGER ZONES

Your Business

As you have grown your business to its current level, have you ever thought anything like this?

1. *The business used to run so smoothly. Now it feels like a constant struggle. What do we need to do to fix it so it operates better again?*
2. *How do I prepare my business and my people so they can take over when I retire?*
3. *How do we get back to the profitability we used to have?*
4. *How do we grow our people into better managers and leaders?*
5. *Our partners don't seem to be getting along like they used to. Can anything be done about this?*

After you have achieved the milestone goal in your business of cracking that first million in revenue, you feel pretty good. This milestone is not easy. 85% of all people in business don't get that far.

However, following this achievement, there are at least four distinct times when underlying issues are also working against you. I have labeled these the *danger zones*.

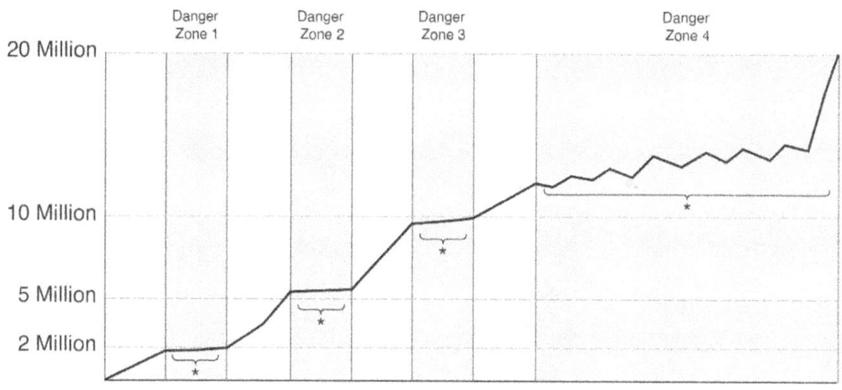

* There are underlying issues lurking beneath each Danger Zone.

The first two major times I have noticed are:

1. As the company approaches two to three million dollars in annual revenue;
2. When the company hits and progresses just beyond the five-million-dollar mark, with the problems often surfacing between 5.25 million and 7 million in revenue.

What are some of the main issues in these first two danger zones?

Danger Zone 1: Approaching Two Million in Revenue

At this size you probably experience, or have experienced, some version of these three issues:

1. You are spread too thin. With too many junior staff to support and not enough senior level help, your problems seem to multiply.
2. You do not yet have the management support in the business that you need. Any senior people in your company are usually specialists—expert in producing results—rather than skilled with managing others. Chances are, managing people is not your forte either. You got into the business as a specialist in your field, not as a manager.
3. Either cash flow is tight, or you are worried about changes in the economy that would put your firm at a cash flow risk. You don't seem to have enough money to plan for and invest in making the changes you need.

Three Million Instead of Two Million?

If you run a project-based firm with larger teams and projects, you may hit these growth challenges at three million rather than two million in revenue.

The key difference lies in team and project size. Interior designers typically work solo or in small teams of two to three people, hitting barriers when approaching two million dollars in revenue. In contrast, architectural firms handling larger projects, each with fees greater than two million spread over a few years, and with project teams of six to twelve people, often reach three million dollars in annual revenue before facing similar challenges. This pattern extends beyond design to construction trades and medical facility companies. Larger project firms using bigger teams typically hit their first major growth hurdle at three million dollars in yearly revenue.

Which scenario better matches your business?

Danger Zone 2: The Other Side of Five Million in Revenue

To grow beyond two to three million in revenue, you must have moved beyond the issues of the first danger zone. People don't grow past this level without figuring how to bring in more seasoned pros to help with project delivery. Further, without some effective assistance in management, things stay stalled at these initial levels.

That's not you. You found a way through. However, have you been caught in the next danger zone?

Just beyond revenue levels of five million dollars, between 5.25 million and seven million, things start to slip again. Your company becomes plagued with more hidden issues. The only question is when exactly they will surface.

Here is a brief summary of some of the common pains at this size. Have you experienced any of these issues?

1. Profits start to dip at this level, for the company overall.
2. Cost overages on projects become a larger issue than ever before.
3. Quality issues emerge, small cracks in what has otherwise been stellar quality and service.
4. Your growth begins to stall out or certainly becomes more challenging to continue, and net income is a constant battle to address.

It is not unusual for a company to start experiencing up and down swings in revenue between five and seven million dollars per year with a consistent and uncomfortably low net income the whole time.

If you are going through this, you know it is not fun at all, and it certainly limits your freedom, dragging you into problems you didn't anticipate. If this period of your business growth has had its ups and downs, you are not alone.

One thing the first two danger zones have in common is that their business owners are still actively engaged in service delivery within the business as craftsmen, or experts in their respective industries. The things that happen in the business feel quite personal and have large impacts on their owners personally.

Stress and tension most often show up here. Part of this is due to an inherent lack of stability that often exists within companies of smaller sizes. Another factor is the pull on your time.

Here's the question you face:

"Do I stay as an excellent practitioner in a profession I love? Or do I move into becoming a business owner? I'm not sure which I want."

At some point between five and ten million in revenue, industry experts who founded these businesses need to choose whether to shift focus from client work to actually running their businesses. This transition can happen in different ways. The owner might step back from client delivery to focus on executive duties. Alternatively, these responsibilities might be delegated to someone else, or they might be shared among a leadership committee. The right approach depends on the specific business and its owner's goals.

One thing is sure. Until this is resolved and a direction is chosen, the feeling of being spread too thin, combined with juggling competing priorities, will continue to limit freedom and add stress and discomfort.

When did this happen for you? Has the stress subsided yet, or are you still in it? For some it takes longer than others.

Are there more milestones? Yes.

Are they accompanied with more danger zones?

Yes again.

Those zones and issues that plague two more levels of a firm's growth come next.

3

SIGNIFICANT GROWTH: THE NEXT TWO DANGER ZONES

AFTER A COMPANY CLEARS THE FIVE-TO-SEVEN-MILLION-DOLLAR hurdle, the next two major milestones where danger zones lurk beneath the surface, ready to strike, are:

1. As the company approaches ten million in revenue, often chewing up bandwidth while impeding growth as early as eight or nine million, and
2. As the company strives for twenty million dollars, specifically in a chasm (think "black hole") that shows up between twelve and twenty million in annual revenue.

More of these *danger zones* will pop up as a company grows beyond twenty million dollars in revenue. It doesn't stop.

No wonder the three levels of freedom are so hard to achieve!

Danger Zone 3: Approaching Ten Million Dollars in Revenue

As your company sorts out the structural issues just beyond five million that eat away at profits and client satisfaction, other issues start to emerge.

These issues are not unusual for companies between eight and ten million dollars. They include:

1. Inconsistency within your project teams' performance in terms of quality of deliverables, project profitability, or both. This is a larger version of the earlier issue, due to a higher number of teams at work.

2. Lack of formal training programs beyond required industry certifications. Your team learns on the job through new projects, and there's no structured approach to skill development.

3. Both staff and managers lack structured support and guidance. You expect excellence but don't provide the tools to achieve it. Despite your team's competence, this sink-or-swim approach undermines their development.

4. Siloed teams start to show up, with protective managers who find ways to keep their people from being "captured" by other managers. You may only be aware of a bit of this. But people will be people. A *lot* more on this to come.

If your business seems to be in an endless loop, hovering just below the ten-million-dollar mark, you may feel the familiarity of these unpleasant issues.

Danger Zone 4: Crossing the Chasm to Twenty Million in Revenue

On the journey from ten to twenty million dollars, you meet the "black hole" that is Danger Zone 4. There is a chasm between twelve million at the low end and somewhere between eighteen and twenty million at the upper end of this frustrating time. Throughout this segment of growth, the issues with the chasm persist.

1. After hitting twelve million dollars, your margins start to drop again. You might see a slow erosion, or it can shift substantially and quickly. This can be scary and is always disheartening.

2. Your management structure is breaking down. Despite having talented people, office politics are intensifying and leadership effectiveness is declining. People who excelled at lower revenue levels now struggle and require more oversight.

3. Partner approvals are increasingly slow and difficult. While you may hold the majority of the shares, forcing decisions without consensus leads to passive resistance and unresolved issues. Or perhaps you have the largest block of shares, but nobody owns the majority. The title of Managing Partner doesn't always translate to ultimate decision-making power. Everyone demands a voice, but competing self-interests make agreement nearly impossible.

4. In this zone, your company is too big for its former infrastructure but too small to profit from the larger

> structures you don't yet have in place. The top leadership members either have competing priorities, or they are lost somewhere in the middle of all the machinations of operating your organization.

If you have been or are in the chasm between twelve and twenty million dollars, you have seen enough to know these issues are common. You have the scar tissue to prove it.

You continue to promise your kids they will see you at their recitals and sporting events. You even plan an anniversary getaway with your partner. But you have the uneasy feeling this is all just a happy delusion.

Does it ever let up?

Summary

As the owner of an expertise-driven business, you've likely faced many of these challenges.

While each company's issues are unique, they all stem from one core truth. Your success depends entirely on your people's skills, expertise, and ability to deliver.

The problems you face evolve as you grow. What started as day-to-day operational headaches have become more serious threats to your company's survival. Many owners stop actively fighting these issues, accepting them as "just the way business is."

It Doesn't Have to Be This Way

Neither high stress nor resignation to the status quo is the answer you want. These growth barriers are solvable with the right approach.

It may or may not be comforting to know that almost all the problems you have dealt with or will face are the same as those faced by nearly every owner of an expertise-driven business.

Is one underlying issue impacting everything you go through?

Yes.

It all comes down to how you see your people.

4

THE OVERLOOKED PROBLEM

As your business grows, you face new challenges—but also new opportunities. Each stage brings different situations that need your attention and solutions. That's just part of building a successful company.

While these challenges get bigger as your business expands, they also push you to build stronger teams and better systems. Learning to handle these situations well is essential for gaining more freedom—both in your business and away from it.

You Get Better

The good news is that as your business grows, you grow too.

Each challenge you tackle builds your skills and deepens your understanding, turning what once seemed like major hurdles into routine problems you know how to solve. This growth in your abilities makes running your company easier and opens new paths to freedom as you become better at leading your organization.

Typical Areas of Focus

As an established business grows revenue through different levels of seven figures and well into eight figures, the focus of owners and leaders tends to be on five key areas:

1. **Business Strategy:** Ensure the company is well-structured for growth and sustainability,
2. **Sales Growth:** Develop the marketing, business development, and sales efforts to ensure revenue continues to grow consistent with company goals,
3. **Service Delivery:** Ensure excellence of operations at the desired profit levels,
4. **Staffing:** Grow the team so each department has proper staffing while growing the capabilities of the people, and
5. **Impact:** Ensure the company is achieving its goals for generating the desired impact outside its walls.

If you, as the leader, focus on these items while growing personally and professionally along the way (that's a mouthful), you can achieve your goals for growth and excellence.

Depending on your size, some or all of these activities have taken your focus as you have grown. But even with clear priorities and strong effort, roadblocks keep appearing. Many business owners come to accept these challenges as unavoidable—the cost of growth.

"That's just the way business is."

The Biggest Concern

Let's assume all of the issues you currently face are properly addressed. Something about size keeps changing the game. You get things figured out at one size. Then as you grow, everything shifts again. It leaves you with an eerie feeling that you are missing something.

This eerie feeling is not an illusion. It is real, and it forms a true threat to the continued growth of your company and to your ability to gain the levels of freedom you desire.

What's going on that makes this so hard? The core issue is not your business.

It is simply how you are looking at it.

Structures versus People? The Big Misconception

As your company grows, systems and structures will become a larger part of the business, no matter what you produce and deliver. It gets to the point, if you become large enough, that you will evolve to 80 percent structures, and 20 percent people. In some service businesses, this may be true with as few as thirty staff members. By fifty people, an under-structured company will feel like an unruly mess.

Even if you are a staunch advocate of your people, it is hard to fight the need for systems and structures. As your company grows, your people present a bigger challenge than any other variable. It feels like herding cats.

Many owners believe they must choose between strong systems or empowered people. But this is a false choice. You can have both. In fact, you must. It is how you work with them that makes a difference.

The Real Choice

Everything and everyone, even people, have and need structures. The difference is whether the structures are there to *control* your people or to *support* them. In other words, is your priority your systems and structures as you grow, or is it your people? You can't cheat and say both. One is always going to win out over the other.

You *control* your "stuff," whether it is a car, your home, your computer, or your TV. You *support* your clients and customers. There's no controlling them.

What about the business itself? The question becomes whether you look at your business as a thing or as a living entity.

Well-Oiled Machine or Intelligent Ecosystem?

Do you consider your business to be a well-oiled machine? Or do you think of it more as an intelligent ecosystem? The answer is not obvious. There are pros and cons to each perspective.

Yet your answer to this question will guide every decision you make as you grow. It will determine whether you have an enjoyable experience or one filled with stress and anxiety. Ultimately it will determine what measure of freedom you generate and how quickly it comes.

Either way, growth will come with difficulties. However, whether those difficulties are bumps and hiccups or major craters depends, in large part, on the outlook you bring to your business, your structures, and your people.

The biggest distinction between a machine and an ecosystem lies in its purpose. Your purpose will give you your focus.

Your Business as a Well-Oiled Machine

The purpose of any machine is to serve you, its owner. It is designed, built, operated, maintained, and evolved for the benefit of owners. Otherwise, why would you own it?

The main appeal of treating your business like a machine is the sense of control it provides — control over how work gets done, how results are delivered to clients, and how you achieve your own goals.

How Your Employees Fit

Your employees are tasked with following the instructions you and your managers provide:

1. To operate the internal machinery (equipment and processes) effectively to generate the desired results the company promises your clients and customers, and
2. To follow the instructions of the managers and senior leaders in response to changes and problems as they arise.

The Goal of Your Business as a Machine—To Bring Predictability to Growth

It is common thinking in business: "People come and go, but the systems and structures are here to stay."

Systems seem to provide the stability in the company, so they become paramount. While people are considered to be important, the systems and structures are seen as a higher priority. After all, there will be more of them as the company grows. At least you have a say in how they work. You have less confidence in your ability to control your people, especially as your ranks swell.

"No problem. I control the systems and processes, and I let them control my people."

If it were any other way, the predictability that you, as owner, want in your organization would be put at risk as the company expands. It is already hard enough to grow a business. There is no need to further complicate it by leaving things to "the whims of your people."

Unintended Consequences

This may have worked in the Industrial Age, when the systems and procedures were clearly paramount. If there is an assembly line, it needs to be followed and kept moving, or everything comes to a grinding halt.

But in a service-based environment, especially one that is driven by the skills and expertise of people, this becomes problematic. The very expertise that your people bring is what generates the desired results for your clients and customers.

If you want the best results from your people, pushing against them in any way will not get you what you want. This includes any attempts to control or constrain them with your systems, structures, and processes.

Your systems approach will yield terrible long-term results.

Think about raising children. The old approach was to control them. But modern parents understand that supporting children's growth works far better than trying to control them. When parents focus on control, they often face years of frustration, often followed by estrangement as they grow older.

Just ask any Baby Boomers or Gen Xers what it was like to grow up feeling controlled. In surveys taken with the generation fondly referred to as Millennials, 83 percent of them named Mom as their number-one hero. Not only that, 82 percent of them listed Dad as their number-two hero.

Back when Boomers were given similar surveys, 40 percent of them said they would be better off without parents.

Employee disengagement, now referred to as "quiet quitting," where people would stay with a company but only put in the minimum effort to satisfy their job requirements, is as high as it has ever been.

1. Only one-third of all employees are actively engaged in their work and their company.
2. Roughly one-third are actively disengaged.
3. In between these two extremes lie the remaining one-third of employees, who consider their employment as "meh."

Ouch!

The machine approach might seem like it will help your business grow. But it often backfires. Your employees will resist being treated like parts in a machine—leading to stress, fatigue, and frustration for everyone involved.

That doesn't sound too promising. Let's see what an ecosystem looks like.

Your Business as an Intelligent Ecosystem

An ecosystem is there to serve all the living entities within it as well as those who are touched by it. This includes owners, clients, employees, contractors, and suppliers.

An ecosystem—effectively a "living system"—operates differently from a machine. It seems to be far less predictable and is much harder, if not impossible, to control.

Think of a forest. Nobody is in charge. Sure, some animals are more dominant than others (just like with people), and those voices need to be considered (again, just like with people).

However, each living organism within the ecosystem plays its unique part. Nobody has direct control over it. In an ecosystem, a form of balance always exists. If something happens at one end, the impact ripples into other aspects of the ecosystem. Everything touches everything else.

That argument may also be made for a business. Actions at one end have ramifications on the rest. It is rare that something occurring in one part of a company doesn't have follow-on consequences elsewhere.

Every living thing within the ecosystem both affects and is affected by all the others.

But if you don't control it, how do you operate it? And why on earth would you invest in it?

The answer lies in a new approach. Forward-thinking companies are discovering that treating their business as an intelligent ecosystem leads to remarkable results.

The Goal of Your Business as an Intelligent Ecosystem—To Tap the Power of Your People for Everyone's Benefit

An intelligent ecosystem is an effective conduit to achieve your goals for your service-based business. The only thing is, many of the rules you have learned to build and grow your business have been based in the Industrial Age model of product-based businesses, where inputs and outputs were predictable. Those rules don't apply to service companies.

What follows is a chart that lists out the differences in a business when treated as a machine versus when operated as an ecosystem, and what to expect in each.

Business as Machine	Business as Ecosystem
1. For whose benefit is it built?	
The owners of the machine	All participants within the ecosystem as well as all stakeholders (including owners, managers, employees, and clients)
2. Who is in control? Who runs it and operates it?	
Owners control it. Owners or their senior leaders and managers run it under the direction of the owners. The staff operate it, following the direction of the managers.	Nobody exerts daily or weekly control. It is more or less self-regulating. Owners and top leaders decide who works there. The operations are left to the teams of knowledge workers, which teams include their respective managers. The owner has a 51% vote on all decisions, but only uses it if needed.
3. What is considered primary?	
The systems and structures that make it work.	All living beings within it, who form each part
4. What is secondary?	
The individual parts of the machinery, including the people.	All parts are primary. None are secondary.
5. What is the purpose of systems and structures?	
To ensure all parts of the machine work, correcting "malfunctions" as needed. This includes ensuring the people do what they are supposed to do since the "non - human" aspects of the machine will operate predictably, per the design.	To support the people within the ecosystem, who bring the systems and structures to life.
6. What is the purpose of employees in this system?	
To operate the machine in accordance with the wishes of the owners. The machinery, supported by people, will generate client results on a sustainable basis.	To work together with each other, using the support structures that are made available. The people who form the ecosystem generate client results on a sustainable basis.
7. What is the role of the manager?	
To direct and oversee the people to ensure they are operating consistent with the intent of the machinery in place.	To act as part of their respective teams, supporting the coordination and operation of the team, and to support team members in their individual and collective efforts to achieve client results. Each team member supports the others as well, as a natural part of the ecosystem.

Business as Machine	Business as Ecosystem
8. What are the consequences for owners in the short to medium predict term?	
They gain a sense or feeling of control due to the predictable nature of machines.	They are often left feeling a bit overwhelmed and out of control due to the lack of predictability of people.
9. What are the consequences for owners the long term?	
They become plagued with continuous people problems that get worse over time, creating the need to constrain people further. This leads to things getting worse again, requiring further systems and structures in an effort to regain the control that keeps slipping away.	They find they can trust their people more. Life gets better and owners regain the fun and joy of their businesses once again.
10. What is the consequence for employees in the short to medium term?	
They are confronted by constraining systems and structures that are designed for the benefit of owners with only limited regard for employees. Some conform despite unhappiness. Others start looking for another job opportunity that is less constricting. A third group starts complaining to other employees behind managers' backs.	They are surprised initially, not knowing if they can trust the changes. It doesn't take long for them to embrace the new arrangements. They go through the process of testing the edges and limits, or to see what's real. Is this just a short--term initiative, or something they can count on over time? If a team-first mentality is accepted and embraced, things continue to slowly improve.
11. What are the consequences for employees in the long term?	
Some employees slow their work down to the bare minimum possible (employee disengagement or "quiet quitting"). Others keep going but start looking for other, less punitive opportunities. Eventually, many leave for better situations and better opportunities. Many of those who stay are people who do not believe they would be successful elsewhere.	As trust builds, productivity starts to creep up — slowly at first and then more strikingly. Over roughly a two-year period, the company evolves to become a better place to work. Outsiders start to become attracted to this organization as a great place to work, learn, and grow.
12. What are the consequences on profits, sustainability, and the return on the investment in employees?	
Overall profits tend to be at lower levels than expected by owners. The business is less sustainable, due to higher employee turnover and lower quality of work. Return on the high investment made in staffing is lower than anticipated or desired. It becomes a frustrating experience for everyone.	Overall profits trend up as employees look for ways to resolve issues while supporting each other, usually through thick and thin, since everyone is a priority within the ecosystem. This becomes is far more sustainable since the mutual benefit of all (including the owners) is the objective. Increased profitability generates higher ROI on the investment in employees.

A Core Business Growth Reality—Outgrowing Your Structures

As you achieve growth in your business, you will invariably outstrip the systems and structures that you previously implemented and that worked at lower revenue levels, as you grow past them to the larger revenue you generate.

The danger zones referred to in chapters 2 and 3 are all based on different structures that have been outgrown as the business expands. The thing that all these zones have in common is that the systems that got the people and the company to a certain level are no longer useful at the larger size. In fact, they actually get in the way of further business growth.

In business, the danger zones also represent something deeper. They are the places where people feel the negative impact of outgrowing structures in the business.

Just like children outgrow their clothes, your business will outgrow its systems and structures as it grows. This happens constantly and will not stop.

When businesses outgrow their structures, owners often react by trying to exert more control over their people. The thinking is simple. Without tight control, you risk losing all control of your company.

But this instinct to control is misguided. Not only does it create resistance from your people, but it actually makes it harder to grow your business.

It certainly does not lead to the freedom you seek.

5

OUTSTRIPPING YOUR BUSINESS STRUCTURES

DON'T YOU RISK LOSING CONTROL OF YOUR COMPANY IF YOU don't control your people as you grow? If you're outgrowing your structures, isn't that the place to focus? How does all of this work as an ecosystem?

Adding People to Your Company

It started off well enough when someone new joined, especially when your business was still in its infancy. At that smaller size, your company functioned almost entirely on individual relationships—those between you and your employees as well as among the employees with each other. When new people joined, they were welcomed. Trust was high. Everyone was out for the same things—the larger objectives of the company—and they tended to work well together since everyone had the same goals.

Even today, the new employees who come on board want this venture to work just as much as the existing people do. Sometimes more. After all, they are betting their future on it. They want to bring their best, and they want to make a difference. This lines up well with the current team, and with you, the owner of this venture.

So, What Happens?

When bringing on new hires, most owners follow a predictable path. Initial training happens, new people get up to speed on their core responsibilities, and then we, as owners, move on.

After all, a hundred other priorities are demanding our attention. The new person seems capable. They'll speak up if they need anything. Right?

And with each new capable person taking on responsibilities, it feels like one step closer to that freedom we've been seeking. One more piece of the business handled. One less thing on our plate.

But here's what actually happens.

The new employee waits for that promised collaboration and mentorship—the partnership that was discussed during hiring. Some of it materializes, but not nearly at the level they expected.

Their boss—whether owner, senior leader, or direct manager—is around less and less. So the new employees do their best, trying not to burden the clearly busy people around them.

And quietly, subtly, their view of both the company and its leadership begins to shift. Even as they work hard to bring value in this unfamiliar environment, that initial enthusiasm starts to fade.

This disconnect between expectations and reality isn't because owners don't care. It's because the daily demands of running a business have a way of overshadowing the sustained investment needed in people's development.

In the Meantime

As the company grows, your job as the boss becomes more complex. It is amazing how quickly the situation flips. With the first shift coming somewhere between eight people and twelve people, the dynamics of your workplace start to change.

When you were an eight-person team, you operated functionally as only one group. Just after ten people, your group naturally splits into two smaller groups. It is hard to hang out with eleven, or twelve, or fifteen others, but a group of four to eight people is relatively easy, socially speaking. This is a natural evolution and part of how people find their place in organizations.

From the perspective of your staff members, "I am more comfortable with my group instead of these other people I don't know so well."

Eventually people find reasons for why those in their group are preferred to, and better than, the other one.

Small, us-them comparisons leak into people's thinking, reinforcing everyone's choices of where they prefer to hang out. This occurs both in the job, where the splits often occur by function, and outside it, where friendships emerge with like-minded others.

With more people, complexity jumps quite quickly, and a bit unexpectedly. This simple graphic shows how much more complexity the addition of new people brings.

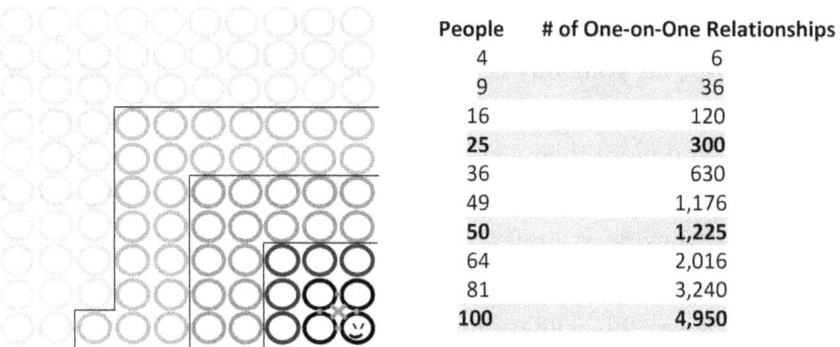

People	# of One-on-One Relationships
4	6
9	36
16	120
25	**300**
36	630
49	1,176
50	**1,225**
64	2,016
81	3,240
100	**4,950**

Figure 5.1: Numbers of One-to-One Relationships in a Growing Organization

With a 9-person company (3 by 3 matrix), 36 different 1-to-1 relationships are present. Moving from 9 people to 16 people (4 by 4) grows that from 36 to 120 separate 1-to-1 relationships. This continues to multiply, growing to 300 relationships with only 25 people.

With 50 people, what you would think of as a manageable size company, there are 1,225 unique 1-to-1 relationships within the company. That's right—well over 1,000. With 50 people, paths cross frequently enough that everyone recognizes each other. While some relationships are closer than others at this level, there's at least a basic familiarity among all staff members.

Then the company grows further, and it gets even more unmanageable. With a company of 100 people, there are 4,950 separate 1-to-1 relationships at play, all at differing levels.

Can you see why a company is so hard to grow? It's crazy.

Each series of relationships brings with it the interpersonal dynamics that are part of being human.

As staff numbers increase, you, the owner, eventually stop being seen as a human being, morphing into this *thing* called "the top boss." Somewhere between 50 and 100 people, you turn from a person into the source of things wanted and unwanted. As you approach 100 people, senior leaders realize they no longer know every person in the company by their name.

The vibe in your business has changed. It feels different from how it used to be. That's because it *is* different. It has become unwieldy and more than a bit overwhelming.

The natural response—and the one we've been taught by dozens of business books—is to resort to using systems and structures to corral the different behaviors of your people.

Otherwise, this situation will get out of hand. That is, if it hasn't already done so.

Addressing outstripped structures seems easy when compared

against dealing with a bunch of people, each of whom has their own agenda, priorities, and ideas of how things need to be done.

When you have to deal with these two forces at the same time (and you do), well, that's something else again.

Growing Staff with Inadequate Structures

Not only have you been outgrowing your business systems and structures, the number of people has also been growing. These two factors compound in unique and unexpected ways.

The consequences of structural inadequacies creep in, sometimes slowly, and often without you or your people noticing until real problems show up. The issues that arise hit the different people in the organization in different ways.

Many of the staff are unfazed by the limitations, finding workarounds for the shortfalls that keep emerging. Yet the job gets a bit harder with each new obstacle, eventually wearing down even your best people.

Other staff members become lost when systems they relied on no longer support their work effectively. What once seemed adequate now feels insufficient for doing their jobs. They do the best they can, but since they are not properly equipped to deal with the new situation, their productivity starts to slip.

Still others treat this as a reason to pull back, until "the boss fixes the situation." Work output slows a bit, and then a bit more.

And what about new people? All they see are holes in what was presented as a coherent organization. Trust is starting to erode already. Not a great start to a new career choice.

This happens again and again with larger consequences at each stage of growth your company incurs.

I hear this from business owners all the time.

"My people used to be great. Not so much anymore, at least for some of them. How can I get them to stop complaining and just do their jobs?"

"I need managers who can get these people productive again. The current setup is just not working. I can understand the need for systems and managers to keep people on track, doing what needs to be done. Most of my people won't do it on their own."

This exact level of impatience adds frustration and will continue to impede your freedom.

An Intelligent Ecosystem

At this point you might be thinking: It's getting harder to run this company every day, and you want me to hand it over to my people to run in some utopian ecosystem? Have you seen who I'm working with?

Hang on.

Let's explore this a bit further to see what's driving what you have now and how to create something more productive for you and your people.

6

WHAT DRIVES YOUR PEOPLE?

"It's all about our people."

Almost every business owner says this. They know it's the right answer. But scratch below the surface and it sure doesn't feel that way to a good number of the people who work there.

Let's dig deeper. Where do structures really fit into your company? And why do they seem to take priority over people so often?

Three key components in your expertise-driven service business make it work:

1. **Tools and Equipment**—The easiest of these to add as you grow is your equipment. Whether it is for an office, a medical clinic or on site in the field, the needs for increased equipment are easy to determine and to address.

2. **Structures**—These include your systems, processes, methods, and any other structures that provide consistency and stability for the organization. If you

grow in any significant way, you will outstrip your structures. Not just once. You will do this again and again. Systems and processes need to be modified to accommodate larger volumes of work. This is trickier than equipment to address, but it can still be done smoothly, once you notice the impact of your growing company on outgrowing these supports.

3. **People**—As you grow, you add people to your organization. After all, it is their expertise you are making available, at least in part, to your clients and customers. As indicated in chapter 5, your people will make life far more complex as you swell your ranks. Each person has their own desires and needs, just like you do, and they rarely align with each other. Your people are where most of your difficulties show up.

Dealing with Problems and Issues

Business owners are a savvy bunch. There are basically three levels of problems and issues you come across in the course of operating and growing your business. Most of them you learn to handle pretty well.

1. **Problems you can see**—If you can see a problem, you can deal with it. Those are the easiest. They may take some effort, especially with complex issues, but if you can see them, you can access the resources and figure them out.

2. **Problems you can't see, but you know exist**—even if you don't see an issue, if you know it exists, you can still address it. It might take a bit more sleuthing, but

you know where to look since the issue is already known to you.

3. **Problems you can't see, and you have no idea they exist**—These are the ones that will cause you grief. Not only do you not see them, but you don't even know to look for them. Instead, you chalk any pain you feel up to what you can see. You end up solving the wrong problem while the underlying issue remains unaddressed.

The core problems and issues that severely impede your growth all fall into number 3. These problems also get in the way of your bid for more freedom.

As you grow your business, you *will* outgrow your structures and systems. This is a simple reality of business growth.

When you can't see the source of a problem (i.e., it doesn't appear to be a marketing, sales, delivery, etc. problem), you figure it must be some different structural issue. After all, you have been told constantly that structures are paramount in business growth strategies. That's even what the experts you have added to your team have taught you.

Are Systems and Structures the Problem?

This is what we think. Too often, it's a misread of the situation.

You do outgrow your structures, and it does cause you and your people pain. This is the symptom you experience. It definitely contributes to the problem, but it is not the source.

The problem is not just structures. The problem occurs when you misread their impact. That is, both their impact on you and their impact on your people.

The first thing that happens when you outgrow your structures is your people's effectiveness starts to drop, while both their anxiety and frustrations increase.

So the real problem is human behavior? At least that's what we think.

Human Behavior

If you ask any business owner what the biggest source of their difficulties is, the answer is almost always people issues. In fact, if you ask them to quantify this, for any business under two hundred people, and frequently for those beyond that level, they will say that people problems form about 80 percent of their issues. And their managers will agree with that.

The bottom line is that people problems are the biggest series of problems a small to medium sized service business faces.

This is what I hear from clients.

1. "How do I get my people to do what I want and need them to do?
2. "What do I do when they fall short?"
3. "I can't fire everyone, or else my business would be a constant turnstile of staff coming and being asked to leave, or leaving on their own, when they see the writing on the wall."
4. "Are you saying I should just fire people who 'misbehave'?"

Or sometimes I hear:

"Just wait a minute. What about the structures? Won't they help?"

Structures versus Behaviors in Business

You have seen or been a part of a business that relies on rigorous structures. This is common with most larger companies.

You have also seen or participated in a business that seems to lack structures. These company leaders don't feel the need for additional structures. They rely on the behaviors of their people for their results.

Examples

1. An Unstructured, Behavior-Driven Company

A small tool and equipment rental business had two locations and twenty staff members. Most employees had been with the company for over a decade, some since the owner Marco first opened the doors. This longevity mattered. With over one thousand pieces of mechanical equipment for rent, deep product knowledge was essential.

The company had few formal policies. Instead, it operated on a simple principle: get customers what they want, when they want it. People learned from each other, and this focus on service became their "secret sauce."

Beyond basic financial and compliance procedures, the company ran on the experience and well-honed behaviors of its people. This approach proved sustainable. Even after Marco's retirement and sale to key employees, the company maintains both its stellar reputation for customer service and strong profits, which are shared through healthy staff bonuses each year.

2. A Highly Structured Company

Another business is a similar size with twenty employees across three locations. Timothy runs these franchised coffee shops with rigorous systems provided by the franchisor.

There seems to be a process for everything, even jury duty. The operation is structured from top to bottom.

Yet despite all these systems, two of Timothy's three locations struggle with basic behaviors—tardiness, poor cleanliness (critical in food services), and general staff apathy. The original location, managed by his wife Lisa, is the only one that performs well.

From this small comparison, it would appear that success and productivity in a business have more to do with staff behaviors than with the structures within.

"Hang on! Are you telling me I have to base the productivity of my business on the behaviors of my people, rather than on systems, processes, and other structures — something I know I can trust? Do you really believe that will give me increased freedom?"

This is a natural reaction. After all, people seem unpredictable compared to systems.

But there's a secret that savvy business owners have figured out: There are structures to behaviors.

And that changes everything.

If you work with a few key underlying factors that shape human behavior, you gain a whole different measure of the effectiveness in your organization.

Many of your problems would be reduced or would dissipate all together. Life in your business would become so much better.

Structures of Behaviors—An Example of One Structure: Past/Present/Future

Many people think that we humans are the collective result of our past experiences, and these experiences shape and drive our future. This may seem right, but it isn't quite the full picture. It leads to misreads all the time.

While your past experiences inform who you are right now, *your perceived future shapes your present.*

If you perceive a brighter future, you are happier in the present. If you foresee a dim or stuck future, or one you fear, your present isn't very happy at all. In fact, if you are like most people, you will become frustrated, disillusioned, or anxious in the present if your anticipated future is feared to be weaker than your current situation.

This dynamic, as part of being human, is as consistent and predictable as gravity is to life on earth.

The elements of human behavior are the critical dynamics that impact each of the issues lurking beneath the milestones of business growth. Not only that, they are also magnified with scale. They get much louder as your business gains size and heft.

The more you understand the impacts of human behavior on your business, the better you will be able to navigate your way through these troublesome zones and enjoy the freedoms you seek —realized in, from, and because of your company as it grows.

Core Dimensions Within Human Behavior

Many preconceived perspectives impact, and often distort, how you see things in your world. By gaining active, conscious awareness of these filters, you make much better reads of your environment and the people within it. This will save you a load of heartache. With a new, wider lens, you are more present to both hazards and opportunities that you never realized were there.

There are filters hard-wired into the biology of every one of us.

If you were to walk down the street and see someone approaching, three things would come up for you unconsciously:

1. Is this person a potential foe? Your primal **biological need to survive** kicks in, ready to protect you from perceived threats.
2. Is this person a potential friend or ally? Your **innate desire to thrive** surfaces.
3. Is this person a potential mate? Your **internal drive to propagate the species** is also alive and actively in gear.

Everyone else you simply ignore. Anything and anyone you see has already gone through these three core human filters before you are consciously aware of them.

In this book, I'm setting aside the drive to propagate the species. That would be the subject of a different book, written by people far more qualified than me.

In looking at survival and thriving, they do have a priority sequence. The biological need to survive is a more immediate driver than the innate desire to thrive. This makes sense. It's hard to thrive if you are no longer here.

Survive/thrive instincts are also why your perceived future shapes your present. You are constantly on the look-out for threats that may come your way as well as opportunities that may present themselves. These survive/thrive instincts are always at work on your behalf.

Driving Influences of Human Behavior

Other than to survive and to thrive, two more features of human behavior are baked into biology, directly affecting every business. Here are four built-in drivers.

1. **Survive.** This core biological need is our first priority in life. If we don't survive, nothing else matters.

2. **Thrive.** We also have an innate desire to thrive. This takes us beyond merely surviving and helps us to find ways of constantly improving our well-being.

3. **Connect**. It has been just over 125 million years since humans were truly independent. Being hyper-social and connected is far safer for people to guard against threats. It also allows us to thrive more effectively. We inherently know that together we are stronger.

4. **Adapt.** We naturally adjust to changing environments, even difficult ones. This built-in resilience helps us navigate everything from personal setbacks—like job losses or breakups—to global challenges like economic downturns or pandemics. No matter what threatens us, humans find a way forward.

Misconception: People Are Logical and Rational

We often see ourselves as rational and logical. We rely on this for all our actions and business decisions. Right?

Well, no.

Humans are not fundamentally logical. Neither you nor I rely primarily on our logic for most of our decisions through each day.

Our decisions are based in our emotions and then justified with logic.

Of course you have logic, and you can reason well. But that's not what drives you, or anyone else, for that matter. The first biological need for humans is survival.

As a mechanism for survival, logic is just too slow.

Humans are primarily driven by emotions. Unlike logic, emotions work very fast.

The thing about this dynamic is that people don't realize the extent that emotions drive our thoughts, feelings, and interactions in life.

For Instance

If a bus is coming straight at me, I don't have the time to think things through. I need to move now! Emotions—fear in this instance—can move me instantaneously. This feature of humanity is immensely helpful to well-being and longevity.

We naturally filter every input through these survive/thrive lenses, both personally and professionally. Most people don't realize how deeply these filters influence our daily decisions and actions.

This hidden dynamic explains why certain growth milestones create so much stress. It's not the milestones themselves. They're just benchmarks. It's how these new circumstances trigger survive/thrive responses in you and your people that matters. When you don't recognize this dynamic at play, you end up building inappropriate structures to eliminate, control, or limit instinctive behaviors rather than working with them. Instinctive behaviors will win every time.

This misunderstanding becomes the source of problems that will plague your business again and again.

Your Business

To increase your facility in dealing with the changing dynamics in your business, you may need more information. First you need to gain a deeper understanding of certain aspects of human behavior, how they really work, and how to interpret the actions of others, and yes, your own actions too. Working with these filters gives you that expanded view.

The more you understand the hidden drivers behind these dynamics, the more effective you will be in operating and growing your own company.

Human Behavior and Changes in Society Over Time

Many significant changes have occurred in the world. In fact, whether we like it or not, things are constantly changing.

"But wait," you say, "with all these societal changes and adaptations, how can I possibly understand human behavior? Everything keeps shifting."

I hear this concern often, especially since the pandemic. Your clients' wants and needs keep evolving. Your employees work differently. Many don't even want to return to the office.

"How do I figure out what makes people tick when everything keeps changing? This wasn't a problem before COVID."

Good News

While many changes have occurred, the underlying elements of human behavior have endured. They are literally part of our wiring. How these dynamics show up in today's business world is a different matter.

The world has changed immensely. People? Not so much.

7

RETHINK THE CORE

When I speak of an intelligent ecosystem, I'm not suggesting some far-fetched, profit-optional dreamland, where you blindly trust your people.

That approach will get you the opposite of freedom in the long run.

The approach I'm suggesting is strategic, pragmatic, and practical to the core. Life in business has changed. Those owners who don't keep up with it will be left to suffer through the journey.

An Intelligent Ecosystem

To address something as complex as an ecosystem, it might be helpful to start with first principles. First principles are the building blocks of algebra, from which most mathematical functions are developed. They work elsewhere in life too.

Elon Musk has been a polarizing man. Like him or hate him, there are things we can learn from him. He used first principles to rethink the common battery. That was key to the development and growth of Tesla. He then proceeded to rethink rockets and propulsion using first principles. He now has SpaceX as well as the Starlink satellite system.

Part 1—Rethink the Core of Your Business

Your business has many moving parts. But what is the core of your business? Or any business?

When I ask people "What is the core of your business?" the common answer I get back is: "Our people." That sounds nice, but based on how I see their companies operate, in most instances this response has very little to do with the reality of what it is like to work there.

Most business owners still treat their people like cogs in a system. Even though most owners are nicer about it than that, and don't even think of it that way, this is often still the reality. The people are subservient to the processes and systems, as well as with the bosses who rule them. Even if the company didn't start out this way, that's how it turns out as you grow.

While expanding your organization, you may have stumbled into the trap of following mechanistic processes to get things done. These processes, when devised, were meant to constrain your people from going "off-script."

This is consistent with the 20th-century industrial "command and control" model, which if you are like most business owners and managers, has been embedded into your psyche. You probably think this way without even realizing it. That's just the way business is. Everything you have been trained on in business includes this "reality."

The reason you wouldn't notice it is because, in your mind, you are not treating your people poorly, like some tyrant would. You are telling them what to do and making sure they do it. After all, there are client deliverables to generate and deadlines to meet. They just need to get on with it and get the job done.

They should know this. Unfortunately, some people need "reminding." The bigger your staff complement gets, the more you seem to need to push for results. It gets tiring, really.

Your people say they love your company, yet your staff turnover is higher than you would like. People keep leaving, taking their talent and experience with them. Whether due to domineering bosses who are hyper-focused only on company results, stringent "guidelines" for every aspect of the work, or employees not feeling heard or appreciated, your best people are choosing to leave.

"My boss is a good guy, usually. But with the latest stresses, things seem to be getting worse. What happened to him?"

Of course, that's not what they say when they are departing. It's usually something else. But those other factors wouldn't have been material if they felt connected within the company. Most employees don't leave—at least not initially. About a third just slow down a bit.

"Why work so hard if the boss doesn't get me?"

Of course, they still act like they are giving the job everything they've got.

That is the way it has been in most businesses, no matter the revenue or the head count. In the 21st century, within expertise-driven companies, a lack of direct focus on the well-being of your people no longer works so well. Fundamentally, we need to rethink the core of our businesses.

What has been the core of the business, and how has it shifted? To address this, let's look to the fundamentals of the business itself.

The Value Exchange

With any business, one of the key elements is a simple but essential concept called the value exchange.

Traditionally there have been two components to this exchange. These two still exist.

1. **Customer Value**—If it's a better deal for me to give you my money, rather than give it to your competitor, or keep it in my jeans, I'll give it to you.

2. **Your Profit**—If it's a better deal for you to take my money and provide your services, you'll do that as well.

This simple notion is the basis of all business.

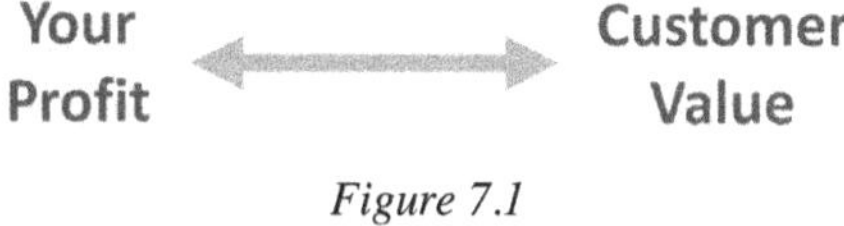

Figure 7.1

If I buy your services, I want a result that your services make available. What you want is the profit from that same exchange.

If there is no value exchange, there is no business… at least not a sustainable one.

The Traditional Core

The core of a service-based company has traditionally been:

Your ability to generate results

Not just any results. The results you need to produce are the ones that will give your clients and customers the value they want. But that, by itself, is not enough. You also need to produce and deliver these results in ways that are profitable to your company.

It looks something like this.

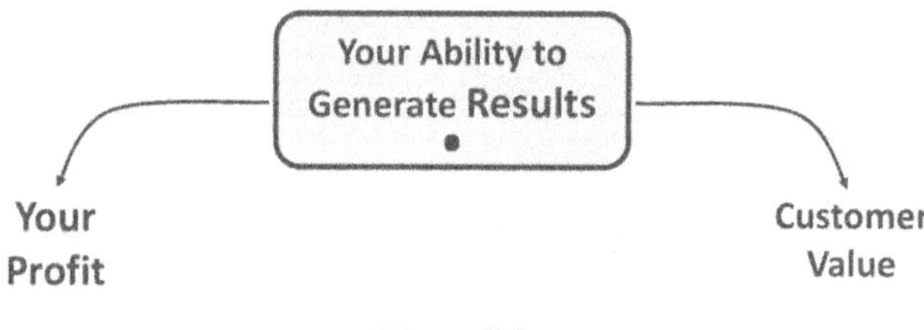

Figure 7.2

Who generates these results?

When you are small, it is an individual team of knowledge workers. At earlier stages of growth, the team is composed of the owner and/or a key senior staff person with the help of some of the junior people as well.

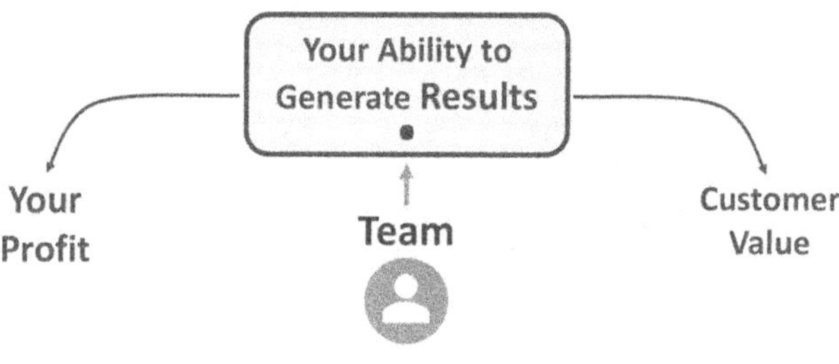

Figure 7.3

As much as you claim they are, your people are not part of the core. They are merely the instruments you direct to deliver on it. When your company is smaller, you may make your people feel like the important parts of the business that they truly are. But that doesn't last forever.

As you grow, you add other teams to handle other client projects. It starts to look like this.

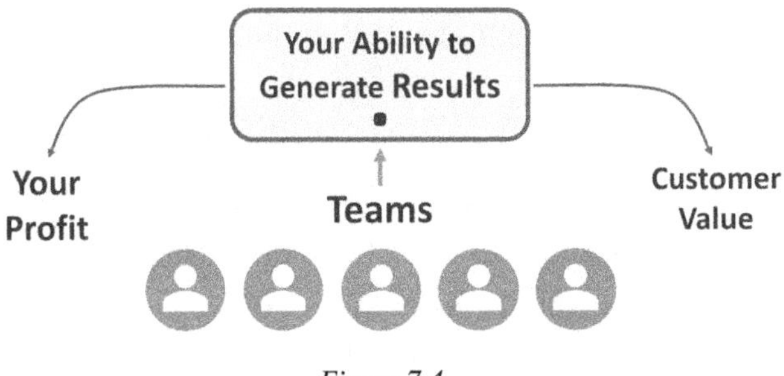

Figure 7.4

As the company grows, the addition of more teams starts to feel unmanageable. Project teams are formed when a new project begins and then broken up when it's completed, only to be reassembled in different combinations for the next project. As the company—and the number of projects—grows, the complexity multiplies. The complexity of working with different people who all seem to need different things, starts to rear its head. There must be an easier way.

One of two strategies tends to emerge. Either the individual project teams continue their cycle of forming and reforming with each new project, or they settle into departments, or teams within industry sectors, based on similar work done repeatedly—either within a discipline or with specific groups of clients. This is where it starts to feel more like herding cats, rather than working collaboratively with a growing number of people across various teams.

"Why can't they just do what we need them to do?"

This is the critical point where the focus shifts—from supporting people to treating them like problems to be solved.

Put another way, this is when the business becomes hard to manage.

The natural response is to start (or continue) relying on systems and structures to ensure the desired results are achieved. These structures are designed to steer employees toward the desired behaviors while thwarting unwanted actions that interfere with client outcomes.

The first levels of this creep in during the initial danger zone, when approaching two million in revenue. By the time you're in danger zone 2 at or after five million, this dynamic is in full force and effect. Without using structures to coral people's behavior there seems to be no way to control the staff enough to achieve the results needed for your clients and customers.

Two Types of Controlling Structures

There are two types of structures you will likely introduce at this point:

1. Controlling Employee Activity

This includes all the systems created to get employees to do what you need them to do, the way you need them to do it. As the saying goes, "People come and go, but your systems and processes are here to stay."

These systems, structures, and processes require your focus and attention to ensure people deliver what's needed, to the required level. Otherwise, your relationships with clients and customers—built on keeping your promises of consistent delivery of predictable value—are at risk.

Ok, so the controlling/constraining structures start to creep in. But what about the employees themselves? How do we keep this a good deal for them?

2. Changing How People Earn Raises

Most growing businesses struggle with maintaining results-based performance reviews and raises. They're just too hard to measure.

With the constant changes that come from increasing staff numbers, the focus often shifts from results to competencies. In response, companies adopt something called "competency frameworks."

Hopefully, these will make things easier.

Competency Frameworks

A competency framework is a tool that measures a preset series of skills, knowledge, and behaviors required to perform a role effectively at a certain level.

Originally designed to measure progress in a variety of areas of skill development within a trade or profession, it has also been used to evaluate employee performance. Competency frameworks are based on the premise that people with similar levels of experience within an industry should have similar capabilities as those of their colleagues.

One the one hand, businesses are paid based on the results they produce for their clients and customers. On the other hand, with all the teams forming and reforming and the focus squarely on projects, it's not so easy to see what results each individual is achieving in their varied roles across different projects. As a result, as businesses grow, they look for an easier way to measure and reward the closest thing to performance they can.

They shift to seeing how strong each person grows, based upon increased competencies in several arbitrary areas that have been selected, often by a professional association, and deemed important for someone's career success. These competencies aren't usually directly linked to the client results of their specific projects.

The model starts to look more like this (or a version of it, with the people broken into their departments, rather than client-facing teams that existed before).

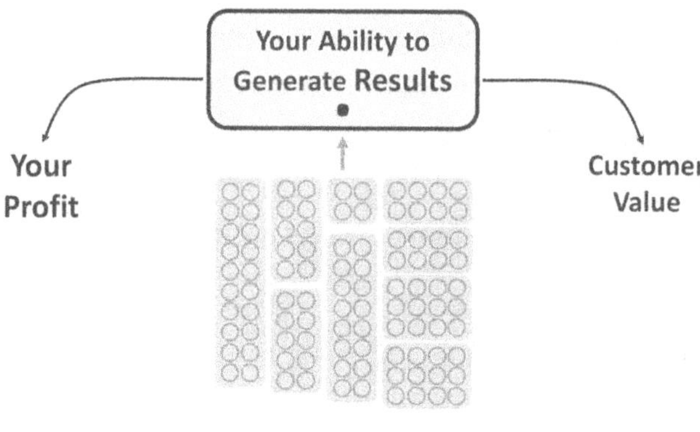

Figure 7.5

If not this, then it's based on teams that are constantly changing according to the needs of each project the company undertakes. Without some sort of competency model, raises become more arbitrary as it becomes increasingly difficult to measure each participant's performance on a given project.

Companies are just not set up to measure everyone's success based upon their respective results.

The Challenge You Face

With the increased complexity of size and continued need to grow your people, it is not surprising that you would move to competency frameworks. This seems like the only way to continue functioning as you grow. People want feedback on their performance, and they don't stop wanting raises. If you can't easily measure their direct performance, measuring competencies seems like a far easier way to justify raises, promotions, or even demotions.

While this shift is underway, you and your people are constantly looking for ways to simplify things. Increased structures, combined with a focus on competencies, seem like the perfect formula. It seemed to work under the 20th-century model—

or, put differently, under the only management model most of us have experienced.

However, simplification begins to shift into conformity. Competency frameworks—especially when paired with more comprehensive systems and required structures—reinforce this approach all too well.

There's one hidden but significant drawback. The minute this shift to conformity begins, companies start to lose their unique advantage—the X-factor of superior performance that comes from the respective strengths of each of their people.

Instead, employees naturally shift their focus from maximizing client results, using what they are best at, to growing their competencies to maximize their pay. Oh, sure. They get through the projects all right. But if pay increases are based on their development of competencies, that is what gets the focus.

The emergence of this mechanistic approach erodes the ability of your people to bring their unique best to your projects. Instead, to get the raises and promotions they want, they attempt to follow your competency-based framework—whether or not it aligns with their unique strengths and best possible contributions to client results.

In European football, called soccer in some places, Lionel Messi is known as the left-footed phenom. He is undersized and not balanced at all. In this sport, traditional logic says your strong foot (in Messi's case his left foot) should take no more than four or five hits in a row before bringing your weaker foot (his right) into play. Otherwise, the thinking goes, the opposing team will know where the ball will be, and they can easily relieve you of it.

In Messi's case, he routinely controls the ball almost exclusively with his left foot, hitting ten to twelve times in a row with that side. Not just sometimes, but all the time. Yet he rarely gets stopped. He is known as one of the best footballers of all time.

That's his superpower. If this habit had been trained out of him when he was young, pushing for well-balanced competencies instead, he wouldn't have become such a strong player.

Each of your people has a superpower—something that makes their respective and collective contributions special. In a small to medium business (under two hundred people), the collection of those powers makes the difference between a solid company and one that is great, highly profitable, and satisfying to work at and to own.

Reverting to competency frameworks for easier control and performance measurement comes at a big cost. As people are asked to conform to some arbitrary norm, the X-factor they bring starts to get lost in the shuffle. The minute your people become interchangeable, you have lost that X-factor completely.

Companies suffer from this all the time.

The Danger Zones

A simple version of this dynamic shows up in some measure as early as danger zone 1. Fortunately, with fewer people, most business owners try to organize teams based on each person's strengths rather than implement a more complex process—when that's possible.

Yet, as you add people, this becomes more challenging.

By danger zone 2 (just beyond five million in revenue), it becomes a real problem. Individual and team performance measures have long since gone by the wayside, other than for the effective completion of the projects themselves. The company has operated without a reporting structure outside of project teams for some time. Eventually, a more comprehensive system becomes necessary, as performance reviews become too burdensome for partners or senior managers to complete without something specific to measure. This typically leads to creating a reporting structure based on departments or functions rather than project teams, since tracking individual performance within project teams becomes too unwieldy.

The new hierarchical structure, while not perfect, becomes easier to administer. Unfortunately, this change further feeds the other issues that show up in Danger Zone 2.

For those who make it past these issues and onto the journey to ten million and beyond, it shows up again, this time in full force, despite any modifications or improvements that have been adopted. If it doesn't hit you in Danger Zone 3, it certainly will in Danger Zone 4, the chasm between twelve million and twenty million in revenue.

The Fundamental Problem

The fundamental problem is that companies begin to move away from—and eventually abandon—the people-based systems they grew up with, which worked so well at lower volumes of work. As managing employee performance across all teams becomes more complex—and consistency harder to achieve—many conclude that project-based teams, as a stand-alone solution, no longer work. So they turn to industry norms.

Having been raised on the Industrial Age model, complete with its competency frameworks, business owners are taught that measuring performance based on growing competencies is the correct approach. According to conventional thinking, nothing else will work.

Remember, no one consciously thinks about the Industrial Age model of management. They just think: management. For longer than we've been alive, management has been defined by this model. It's all we've ever known.

Rethinking the Core—A Different Approach

What alternative way of operating would still allow you to tap the power of your people, for both the employees' and company's benefit?

The fact is, you already have part of the framework—and you know it works well, at least at a smaller scale. You just need to refine it and add a few components to support growth.

The key to success has always been and continues to be to tap the expertise of the individual teams of knowledge workers, collaborating with each other to generate the desired results.

After all, that is where the complex work for clients gets done.

In a product-based business that is carried by larger systems—like assembly lines—the people may merely be conduits. However, in a service-based business, or in any business where the expertise of the people is required, they are part of the core of the business, not a fad or add-on to it.

In short, your teams of knowledge workers are part of your core, not merely a conduit to achieving the core results. You need to treat them this way.

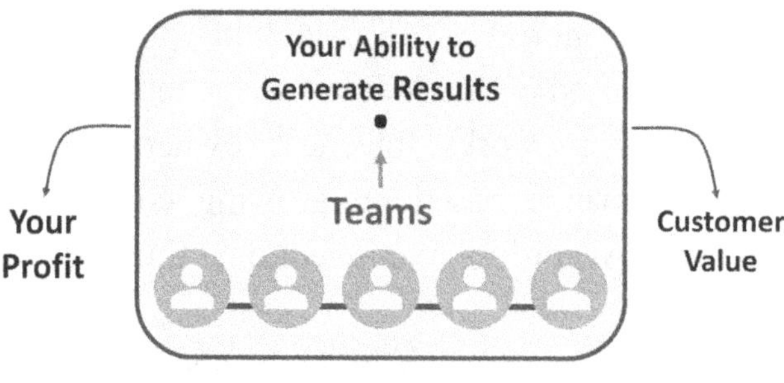

Figure 7.6

Only if people are considered as a fundamental part of the core will they continue to get the support they need to ensure your business will flourish.

Your people, working in teams, generate those results that your clients value. These people are core to the very existence of your organization.

Each individual doesn't need to have the same list of competencies as everyone else. Collectively, the team needs all the skills at the table, but no single person is required to have them all. A model based on complementary strengths addresses this concern. You already do it to an extent in your project teams. Now it's time to make it a core part of your company. This approach takes the pressure off your people to morph outside of their expertise just to qualify for their next raise.

Instead, each person brings their unique talents and abilities to the table to generate results in their respective areas. They get to bring what they do best, which has proven successful so far in their careers. This tends to be what lights them up, benefiting not only them but the whole team as well. What would serve the company best is to support each person to grow their respective superpowers to contribute to the team.

With this perspective, individual teams of knowledge workers are back to focusing on achieving client results rather than merely building an arbitrary list of desired competencies that everyone must possess.

Using this approach, you will be better positioned to tap the unique and growing skills of each person on each of your teams. Further, you can keep the focus on growing the company's ability to generate the results clients seek from you. With this, and some other organizing aspects, your business may once again be positioned to grow effectively and more profitably for everyone.

Rethinking the core is an essential cornerstone of growing and nurturing an intelligent ecosystem. When combined with other elements, this will lead to more freedom. But to do that safely, you need to make and keep the right deal with those you are planning on bringing into the heart of your business—your people.

Otherwise, any attempt at change will turn into a very bad idea.

8

THE SOCIAL CONTRACT

SIMPLY CLAIMING TO INCLUDE PEOPLE AS PART OF THE CORE OF THE business doesn't make it true. Nothing is coming from this arrangement specifically for them.

What key elements drive staff productivity and loyalty?

The Social Contract Between Employers and Employees in the 21st Century

The tacit agreement between companies and their people has changed from the 20th century model to today. It used to be transactional in nature. You do a job for me, and I pay you. There were rare times when it was more than that, but in most cases, it boiled down to straight services for pay.

Now it is far more nuanced, especially in businesses where expertise is involved. We need partners and close allies, not just transactional operators. Without an upgrade in the depth and quality of the expertise and character of our people, any hope of gaining more freedom on a sustainable basis vanishes.

The social contract is vital to develop functional relationships with teams of knowledge workers. These are the people who deliver the promises made to your clients.

What does each party get in this social contract? Each party comes to the work environment expecting to gain four specific things.

What the Owners and Company Expect to Gain

The expectations you now have of the people you hire include:

1. Generate individual client results

They are expected to learn the role and produce something that measurably moves client situations forward. As their skills increase, they are expected to provide more value to clients while growing in their profession or trade.

This applies whether it is a medical assistant conducting and completing the patient intake process, or a marble installer learning the precision measuring tools for accurate stone cuts and installation of a countertop in a luxury home.

Staff members are each expected to be able to produce and generate individual client results, either immediately or as new skills are learned.

2. Work together to generate collective client results

In a medical clinic, team members work together to create an effective and consistent patient experience. Each person —from the physicians to the clinical staff—has specific responsibilities that complement the others. For example, while one team member manages patient flow, another prepares examination rooms, and others focus on direct patient care. This coordination ensures the best possible care, delivered on a timely basis.

Similarly, in the stone and tile business, installations require coordinated teamwork. One person may handle precise measurements while others manage the cutting and installation of heavy materials. Each team member brings specific expertise—whether in cutting techniques, material placements, or installation methods. Together, they complete complex projects with heavy, yet delicate materials that no individual could manage alone.

3. Develop a stronger corporate culture

This is the result of numbers 1 and 2. When people learn and work both individually and together as part of a team, it generates stronger client results. This practice leads to the development of a powerful culture, based in contribution, both to each other and for the benefit of the company's clients and customers.

Within a medical clinic the collective priorities may be:

1. A mutually supportive environment, both with fellow staff and with patients who visit,
2. Speed, accuracy, and attentive care, both during visits and in follow-ups that occur within a day of each patient visit, and
3. Having people who visit to feel seen, heard, and nurtured back to health.

With a stone and tile sourcing and installation firm, the collective priorities may include:

1. Precision, combined with attentiveness to clients and other trades on site,
2. Strong commitment to a clean environment throughout a job,
3. Stellar results, and
4. A mutually supportive environment with others in the company.

"I want to know that you have my back as we work together. I in turn, will have your back as well."
This is part of what the owners and leaders of a company want to see happen.

4. Progress toward the company's larger purpose
The 4th element is the culmination of the first 3. Through the collective actions and delivery of results from everyone, progress is made toward the larger purpose of the company.

A medical clinic might have the purpose of contributing medicine and care in underserved markets at comparable levels of service to the best clinics in the country.

Whereas a stone and tile company might have their purpose to improve home and commercial environments.

Those are the things expected by you and your managers of the people who join your teams. What about individual employees?

What Individual Employees Expect to Gain

1. Compensation

The money doesn't have to be the best on the market, but it does have to be reasonable for the job at hand. Some professions and trades have well-established norms for rates of pay within different industries and markets. You don't necessarily need to pay the most, but you do need to pay appropriately.

You have to get the money right.

2. Professional training and growth

In skilled trades, professional services, or other services where expertise is required, your people also want to gain both initial and ongoing training and career growth. This is an active part of their expectation.

This is not just initially or at junior levels. People have the expectation that this will be provided throughout their careers and at all levels within the company.

3. Access to meaningful work

In a learning environment of growing expertise, every job has the potential to be meaningful. Even the "boring jobs" become meaningful if there is consistent access to learning and the ability to turn that learning into professional growth.

In many jobs, the "learning by doing" part is more important than the pay, as long as the compensation is not out of line.

The active daily commitment to learning through the work itself brings new meaning to the tasks at hand.

4. Access to develop meaningful relationships

Connections between people grow when they are working together toward a common goal. The shared challenges, successes, and daily interactions create bonds that strengthen over time.

In their work with colleagues, clients, and other professionals, these relationships become increasingly meaningful. They often become a primary reason why people stay with a company, even when other aspects of the job may be less than ideal. The strength of these professional relationships can outweigh many workplace frustrations.

The key factor in each of these two lists is the second point. Bosses need people to work together to generate results that one person could not produce on their own. Employees actively expect their employers to provide training and development that advances their careers to progressively higher levels.

The Social Contract Summarized

Owner/Company	Individual Employees
1. Generate individual client results	1. Compensation
2. Work together to generate collective client results	**2. Professional training and growth**
3. Develop a stronger corporate culture	3. Access to meaningful work
4. Progress toward the company's larger purpose	4. Access to developing meaningful relationships

We have already established the need to bring people into the core of the company. Now we understand what both the company and the employees are expecting out of this relationship, especially with the focus on the second point on each side of the above table.

This makes the training and ongoing growth of people a critical part of successfully growing a company.

Revisiting the Value Exchange

To make this change meaningful and not merely lip service, the value exchange must fundamentally change in how it operates within companies.

The fact is, the value exchange has shifted in our post-pandemic world. The only question is whether companies recognize the shift and decide to work with it.

In an expertise-based services company, the employees, those teams of knowledge workers, need to be a fundamental part of the value exchange. That's the only way they will contribute sufficiently to be part of the core of the business.

The picture of a modified value exchange now looks like this:

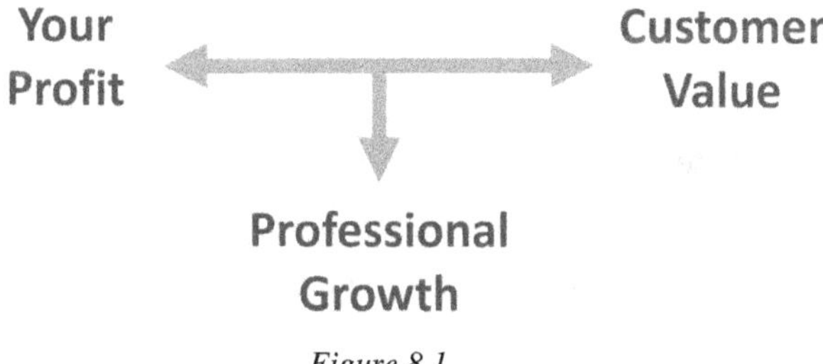

Figure 8.1

The New Addition—Professional Growth

This is for everyone throughout the organization, including you, the owner. Without a real commitment to learning and growth, the culture won't permeate through all levels of the company.

With it, you create a powerful culture where all sides of the social contract are served.

The new version of the value exchange is consistent with the changes in staffing that have been occurring in the market. It also lines up with what makes life in business easier to manage as the company grows. It is instrumental in growing your freedom.

The revised expression of the core of the business and the updated value exchange feed into what your people want in their work in the 21st century.

Differing Opinions

I find people's attitudes about the social contract to be fascinating. Some business owners with whom I have shared this notion not only accept it, they say, "Of course! It only makes sense. You are stating the obvious."

Others give this lip service, acting like it is true, but they don't really believe it.

An Example

I had one architect, a newer partner with an established firm, retort, *"I became an architect to make a positive impact on the landscape of our city. I didn't become a professional to babysit a bunch of newbies. I'll work with people, but don't ask me to change my focus from architecture to growing them. They should learn by doing, just like I did."*

An interesting point with this person is that even when she made that statement, she was outwardly presenting herself to others in her firm as one of the most staff-centric people within her company. With those secretly harbored thoughts, is there any question about why the adoption of an employee-centric framework had difficulty taking root?

This firm's partner eventually warmed up to the idea of the importance of her people and their growth. Despite her privately stated opinion, she did see the value of growing her people and sought out how to accomplish this. Over a very short time—nine months—she grew to become one of the strongest leaders in developing the people within her project teams.

What shifted for her? She loved sharing her own love of the industry with the more junior people, especially those who took pride in their commitment to support the growth of the profession of architecture. They shared her enthusiasm, so she had all the time in the world for them. It didn't hurt that she connected with a latent inner desire to see others around her grow and prosper as well.

This speaks to the power of meaningful work and meaningful relationships in the development of someone's career.

Entrenched Attitudes and the Clash of Different Generations

The highest-ranked senior partner in a multi-state, USA-based engineering firm with over 400 professional staff also pushed back.

"We all learned by being thrown in the deep end and having to work it out. We turned out fine. That's what we should do with everyone who comes in. Otherwise, we won't know what mettle they bring and whether they can withstand the challenges in our profession."

This is merely another twist on the 20th-century business mentality. Thankfully, most of the other people in that firm were more forward-thinking than this person. Knowing he won't change, his partners are quietly awaiting his retirement within the next few years.

While many leaders are adapting to new workplace dynamics, some remain committed to traditional industry approaches that shaped their own careers.

As I've worked through these changes within companies of all shapes and sizes, I've seen different responses to these changes that tend to fall along generational lines.

Many Boomers and older Gen-Xers reside on one side of the spectrum. They tend to want everybody to just do what they're told, like they had to do when coming up. These groups grew up in the time of the Industrial Age model. That was and is just as prevalent to them as the natural tendency to use your dominant hand in writing. It is considered to be "just the way it is." This is what I experienced too—not only in my observations of friends and colleagues but in what I went through with some of these same challenges.

Gen Zers coming straight out of school are on the opposite side of the spectrum, having been raised as "customers" of their school system. They were raised to believe they were just as important as anyone else, child or adult. Entering the workforce, can feel like a rude awakening when confronted by attitudes far different from how they were raised.

Wary of more senior counterparts at work who don't show appreciation for who they are and the potential they hold, Gen Zers tend to want their side of the contract but many don't yet think enough about the company/client side.

Millennials are able to bridge this gap since they were raised similar to Gen Zers but have been in the workplace longer. They have learned and understand the primacy of client relationships. They also possess a real appreciation for what it takes to develop the expertise that their more senior colleagues have acquired.

Closest in age to their younger counterparts, Millennials appreciate what Gen Zers are going through as they try to navigate their way in the world of work, having been there recently themselves. Many Millennials bring more compassion to this new generation than their older colleagues. As a result, they become true allies, incredible mentors, and effective resources to this newest generation of talent.

Mutual Importance with the Boss?

An underlying issue has faced employer-employee relations for centuries. *"I'm the owner. I have the wealth and the jobs to give out. If you want to keep yours, you need to listen to me and do as I say."*

The problem with this, though, is you are not running a McDonald's restaurant—often thought of as similar to the Industrial-Age assembly lines—where you can easily replace anyone with anyone else.

When you lose an expert or budding-expert knowledge worker, all of that expertise and experience is extremely hard, and potentially expensive, to replace.

Now employees are saying, *"We bring the knowledge, the know-how, and the breadth of capacity that no single owner can bring. We deserve a voice at this table too."*

Treating owners and managers with respect and importance, while treating each employee with the same, is key to developing an intelligent ecosystem.

Done properly, this forms the seeds of a far healthier series of relationships in business. It becomes true only if you, as the owner, accept this thinking and if your people bring their respect for what you provide, not just their own contributions.

Employees need to accept this way of thinking as well to create real balance. As new ways of thinking and operating become part of the culture, your company truly shifts from a machine to an intelligent ecosystem. Each person is considered to be important to the success of the organization and in their own right as well.

Sound utopian or like some unrealistic fantasy? It's not.

It merely aligns self-interests where there is common ground. Having and using power over others has never been the most effective way to get things done. It leaves too many negative residual side effects within interpersonal relationships. Working together works so much better.

Working with the Expanded Core

By expanding the core of the company to include the individual teams of knowledge workers and skilled trades who generate results for clients, it changes the view of the organization's people. Instead of being viewed as cogs in the system, people will naturally be treated as partners and allies in generating the desired results.

Rather than a human robot, who is subservient to the boss, the people bring their thinking, creativity, and different experiences and perspectives to the problems that need to be addressed.

Considering one team for a moment, you have this:

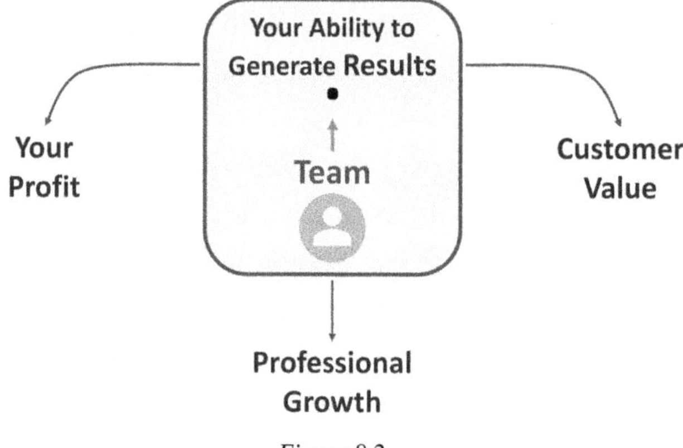

Figure 8.2

The team is the group whose ability to generate results counts. The people in today's workforce are unwilling to merely be cogs in a system. This is especially true for those of the two most recent generations. They want to be treated as part of an ecosystem, where their voices count too.

This is where the social contract comes in.

By tapping the second point on each list, the boss wants results that are larger than any individual can create on their own. Employees each want training and growth to evolve their careers.

The development of an intelligent ecosystem is critical in the 21st century to gain the freedom you seek. The social contract is a key structure in supporting that ecosystem.

That said, this structure doesn't work with just anyone. One of the most critical factors is who you bring into your company. After all, they are at the core of your business.

9

HIRE SMART

YOUR FREEDOM GROWS WITH THE QUALITY OF YOUR PEOPLE.

If you get the right-fit people in your doors, that's literally half the battle.

Think of an orchestra. You can have people feel special and have them work really well together. But if they aren't great musicians, each specializing and excelling with their own musical instrument, then at best, the orchestra will only be mediocre.

Mediocre performance from your people will not gain you the freedom you want. The right people will increase your freedom while the wrong ones will keep you trapped.

It starts with choosing who should be in your company. Getting the right people onto your teams is half the job of gaining freedom. The other half is what you do once they are there. We'll cover that part later.

One of the biggest frustrations I hear from business owners is they cannot find the right people for the roles they want or need to fill within their company.

Have you encountered this issue in your business?

Two Problems with Hiring

There are two fundamental, yet often overlooked traps you or your team will likely fall into. They are:
1. Not aiming high enough, and
2. Saying yes to someone out of desperation, even though you know they aren't a great fit.

Attracting the right-fit people is less about who's available and more about your perspective on recruiting and selection.

When you are counting on the expertise of your people, the relationship changes.

I haven't met anyone who wants subpar performers as employees. However, we also don't want to overspend for talent. We don't mind paying appropriately for the right-fit candidate, but throwing more money at people doesn't have a direct link to getting a better person. Anyone will take more money if offered.

Most business owners end up lowering their standards when the right person doesn't appear quickly enough. They settle for someone who's not quite the best fit, convincing themselves that "good enough" might work.

"Better this person than nobody," we tell ourselves.

However, with each of these decisions, our company gets harder to operate. The difficulties can't be attributed to one person or another. All the concerns expressed and push-back on initiatives will seem to make sense.

However, what emerges is one of three things.

1. **Uneven performance and dissent**. A culture of quiet complaints about broken promises and lack of support emerges. There's no uprising—just a low-level dissent

as people try to succeed in what they perceive as a broken system.

2. **Bare Minimum Effort**. People work until quitting time, not a minute longer. Initiative disappears. No one goes above and beyond when extra time is needed. It's not one person. It becomes the general feeling.

3. **Passive Dependency**. People wait for instructions and do exactly what is asked, no more. They wait to get directions from bosses before anything occurs. Everyone expects the boss to do the thinking. This also spreads throughout the company.

There are variations of these three behaviors, but these generate the main underlying issues that evolve when you "take the best of the bunch" and try to work with them.

Clearly, something is not quite right here. So, what can you do?

If you want great people, you may need to aim higher than you have been until now.

To find and come to agreement with right-fit candidates for positions within your company, there are three things to consider. They are:

1. Raise your standards,
2. Get clear on what you want, and
3. Get to know them before hiring.

Raise Your Standards

Only hire potential partners or close allies. This is probably a higher standard than you have been holding. After all, you only need someone to fill this role (fill in the blank). Instead of accepting the minimum standard you can find, it's time to raise the standard.

Stop settling for "the best people we can get." Aim higher.

Never add someone based on a traditional transactional employment arrangement.

I can hear it now, "If I can't find the right people with a low standard, how am I supposed to find them with a higher standard in place?"

Your standards will change who you look for, how and where you look, who you accept, and who you will not accept on your staff.

With different eyes, you see differently. In my experience over three decades of supporting business owners to grow their companies, this can be done. In fact, we do it all the time.

There are three actions I have seen countless times that support these efforts.

1. **Change Your Approach.** Set things up to attract a higher caliber person.

2. **Be Patient but Optimistic**. It may take you longer to find the right-fit person for your team. However, I am frequently surprised to find that with higher standards, the right people seem to start showing up far earlier in the process than expected.

3. **Trust the Process.** You will find the right-fit person for your company eventually, unless you short-circuit the system by taking a "close enough fit" (read near-miss) candidate at any point in the process.

The difference in hiring potential partners and/or close allies is in the attitudes of the people you hire. Skills may be developed.

Character is a completely different matter. It is a much longer process to develop the attitude and outlook needed to succeed and excel in the role and with the company. Think in terms of years, not weeks or months.

A. Hiring Right Is Half the Game

Literally, one half of the process of growing an effective, service-based business lies in hiring the right-fit people for your organization. If you only take on people who would qualify as either a potential partner or a close and trusted ally, things slowly start to get better. To the right-fit candidate, the job is about much more than tasks completed. It's about generating results, growing their career, and contributing to the larger purpose of the company.

You can take this approach with anyone at any level of your company. For instance, you could take on someone who has just finished school. If their attitudes and outlook are strong and align with your values, that is a good start. If not, keep looking.

Yes, really, even for new graduates.

If you think it's impossible to get the right people, this opinion will cost you. Even if you already have one hundred people, and you need twenty more, twenty of the right-fit people are out there for you to find. You just need to use more creativity.

I know this is easier said than done. That's why I've provided our complete hiring guide.[1] Merely go to FreedomBookResources.com to access this guide.

You have been creative enough to get your business this far. You've got this!

You want people who bring accountability for both individually generated and collective team results. You know it.

1. For free access to our complete hiring guide, please go to FreedomBookResources.com

They know it. You and your teams will naturally treat each other with the respect associated with having such highly regarded people working alongside them and you.

And with this not-so-small point, the stakes get higher.

Increasing the standards and the requirements for a candidate to hurdle the bar of "potential partner/close ally" is more rigorous. The good news is the process doesn't need to take much longer.

When hiring those special people for your team, what do you consider?

B. Get Clear on What you Want

You will look for several skills and attributes when seeking to add people to your team. You want them to have:[2]

1. Job-related skills and attributes,
2. Attributes that would help them fit with the manager and with the team,
3. Attributes consistent with your core values,
4. Seven A-Player attributes[3], and
5. Ten management attributes[4], if management is part of the job, either now or in the future.

Six Key Attributes to Seek Out in Expertise-Based Industries

For a company that requires growing expertise of teams of people, in addition to the usual items listed above, you will need six specific attributes to be present:

---

2. For more information, please go to FreedomBookResources.com
3. These A-Player attributes are within the free hiring guide at FreedomBookResource.com.
4. These ten management attributes are in the free hiring guide at FreedomBookResources.com.

1. Clear thinking
2. A voracious hunger to learn and grow
3. An inquisitive, curious mind
4. Humble outlook
5. A commitment to contribute to others
6. Allowance for the contributions of others

1. Clear Thinking

Someone who is clear thinking works better in an expertise-driven environment. Some people have book smarts. Other have street smarts. Clear thinking is always part of the picture. I have met people who aren't necessarily the most articulate, but if you put them in front of a project, they can see and comprehend patterns that others miss. This places them ahead of the pack. Beware of muddled thinking.[5] This can be a real setback to any company or team.

2. A Voracious Hunger to Learn and Grow

Everyone claims to want to grow. Unfortunately, for many it's simply posturing to get the job. These people, while claiming to learn, are more interested in demonstrating how much they know.

On the other hand, an excitement about the future, combined with an eagerness to learn and grow into it, fits what you want in your people. The results these people

5. Muddled thinking is very costly to an expertise-driven company. However, it is not difficult to spot within a well defined hiring process. Please go to FreedomBookResources.com for the full hiring process. This process contains components that will help you to uncover muddled thinking, in addition to other valuable resources.

generate continue to expand and evolve. So too does their career.

3. An Inquisitive, Curious Mind

Related to learning is an inquisitive mind. One of the most powerful emotions in life is curiosity.

For curiosity to exist, we need two things to be present:

1. You can't already know, and
2. You have an active interest to find out.

When people are curious, they tend to dig a little deeper, go a bit further, and discover things the non-curious might overlook or miss.

This is essential for people who want to grow their expertise and their results.

4. Humble Outlook

People who think they are better than everyone else don't tend to do too well in expertise-driven fields, except as mercenaries—"hired guns." They may excel at their craft or profession, generating individual results, but a lack of humility shows up in their views of others on the team.

Beware of these people.

Without humility, a need to be seen as better than others is almost always present. This tendency works against effective teamwork and the larger results of their team.

Humility allows for growth and contribution to larger

objectives of the whole team or organization, not just an individual's agenda.

5. A Commitment to Contribute to Others

When growing as part of an expertise-driven team, a passive willingness to contribute is not enough. It needs to be part of the natural way someone operates. If this way of operating is absent, things eventually unravel, getting progressively worse. It's just a matter of time.

As anyone who has participated in team sports knows, one team of five people works far better than a series of five people—even stars—each putting in their respective solo efforts. An active commitment to each other makes real, tangible impacts on effectiveness. Why?

Without an active commitment to contribute, things become transactional. I'll only do this for you if you do that for me. With the ebbs and flows of any business or project (or for any team), things are rarely equal across all the people at any single point in time. A willingness to jump in and help others, regardless of the return, is the only way a team can work at its best consistently.

6. Allowance for the Contributions of Others

If someone doesn't have a natural inclination to allow for other people's contributions, they tend to get defensive and block or misconstrue what otherwise might be helpful input. This often leads to people becoming siloed and competitive with each other in a destructive way.

Friendly competition can be fun. Blocking other people's

contributions isn't fun for anyone. That's when everything gets harder. This issue gets in the way of collaborative work.

On the other hand, a group of people works much better when each person is comfortable with working as part of a team. A team-centric mind-set requires a commitment to contribute to others and to allow for other people's contributions to them. Teams with these people do much better. An allowance for the contributions of others is key to building well-functioning teams.

The good news is that this allowance for others' contributions is pretty easy to read in an interview if you are looking for it.

C. Get to Know Them

It's nice to have all these criteria. It's even more powerful to use them in the hiring process.

The biggest thing you need to do is to genuinely get to know people, even as they are applying to work for your firm. Taking the time, over multiple interviews will ensure you the opportunity to understand what applicants are about. This time also helps to determine the potential fit between your candidates and the company, as well as their ability to do their specific jobs. If you go to the link FreedomBookResources.com, you will have access to a sample of our complete hiring process, with all the questions and expected responses, as well as how to analyze candidates. Enjoy!

By hiring smart, including ensuring these six elements are present, and taking time to really get to know people before you invite them into your company, you will be able to set a proper foundation that builds teams in a positive, productive, and rewarding direction.

This is crucial if you truly desire to gain more freedom.

The next piece of building an intelligent ecosystem is to utilize a system of training, growth, and support for your people within your growing company.

10

TRAIN AND GROW PEOPLE

HIRING SMART IS CERTAINLY HALF THE GAME OF CREATING AN intelligent ecosystem. The other half includes several factors. One of the biggest of these is the professional growth and development of your people through the course of their careers.

This has a direct, positive impact on your ability to gain more freedom as your business grows. To recap, the three levels of freedom are:

1. To gain freedom *in* your business so you can choose the focus of your own efforts. The more you support your people to increase their expertise and depth, the more choice of focus and freedom you gain.

2. To gain freedom *from* your business, you need to equip your people with the skills and expertise to continue to serve your clients without needing you constantly at their side.

3. To increase the freedom *because* of your business, the asset value and impact your organization provides must expand without your direct inputs at the production level.

All of these are positively addressed with the professional growth of your people.

Training and Growth from Your Perspective

Owners hire people to work together to generate the results that your clients and customers want.

Everything a business generates is designed to directly address one of the three elements of the value exchange:

1. Increase customer value,
2. Protect and grow profit,
3. Contribute to the professional growth of the people within the organization.

To work in your business, the people need to deliver one or more of these three elements. That, specifically, is why you hire the people you do.

Some contribute to these results directly. Others have a more indirect contribution. Whether direct or indirect, each person's contribution needs to move forward customer value, company profit, or the growth of the people within your business.

Training and Growth from the Perspective of Your People

People in expertise-driven businesses want to become better at what they do. They want to master skills that allow them to grow in their career and profession.

Unless both your perspective and theirs are met, nothing will be sustainable. If, however, both can be achieved, you have solid progress on developing and growing your intelligent ecosystem to serve all.

Remember the social contract we discussed in chapter 8? If you look at point number 2 of what employees gain, there is a promise to support their training and growth.

But training and growth in what?

The Ability to Generate Results

The promise of employers regarding their people's growth is specific. The growth promised is to help them develop the ability to generate results that the company produces. All results will be either directly or indirectly in service of the three elements of the value exchange.

There are four dimensions of those results:

1. **Technical Results**—based on the company's expertise,
2. **Financial Results**—to generate results that are fiscally feasible and cost effective,
3. **Human Results**—to make it easier to work with each other and build stronger relationships with clients and customers,
4. **Sustainable Results**—to generate them without wearing people out or unnecessarily using up other resources that will be needed to flourish over a longer period.

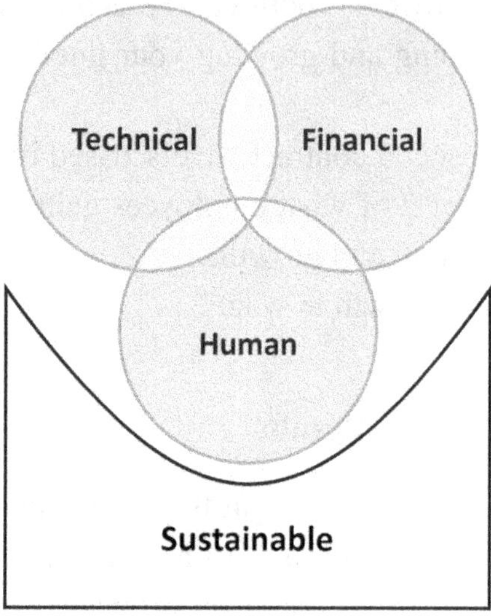

Figure 10.1

While these results are focused on client deliverables, there is plenty there for people to learn from you, from your leaders and managers, and from each other.

To arm people with the ability to generate client results, both individually and as part of the team, two tools are useful:

1. The job role of each individual, and
2. A growth plan for each person on the team.

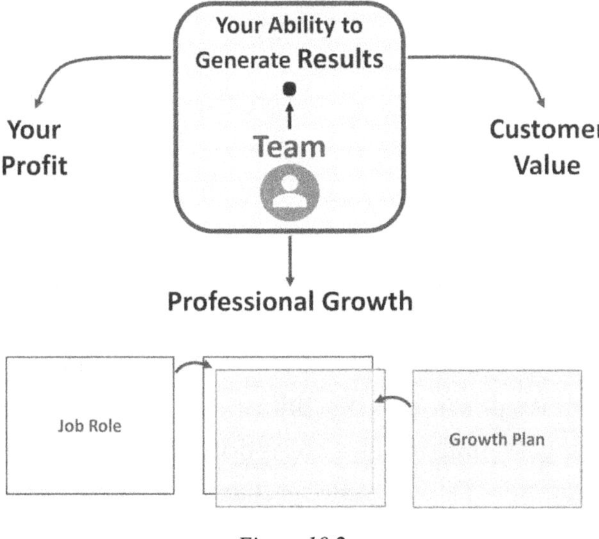

Figure 10.2

The Job Role

The job role[1] includes two key elements at the first level:

1. The purpose of the role, and
2. An overview of the top three to five areas of accountability for a person's job.

Purpose

Every job exists to generate a result. What result does the person in this role need to generate? By clarifying this in one sentence, the purpose of the role becomes clear.

1. There is lots of detail on the job role, including examples, in our free hiring guide, which you can get by visiting FreedomBookResources.com

Three to Five Areas of Accountability (Job Chunks)

In the second part, lay out the areas where employees need specific results to succeed in achieving the purpose of their role. This gives an employee further clarity as to the scope of their focus. Within each of the areas identified, further results may be needed as well.

Having a series of job requirements is not new to companies or to employees. Some version of this forms the basis of most jobs that have been defined within a firm. However, instead of listing twenty or thirty different tasks, duties, and activities within a job, I strongly suggest limiting the description to three, four, or five areas of accountability. This is called "chunking." For those who need them, the details of those twenty to thirty tasks can always go inside each respective area of accountability.

By starting with this overview perspective using job chunks, the job becomes both more strategic—focusing on results from a higher level—and also far more manageable to achieve. This approach makes it easier to keep the focus on the things that matter, such as achieving the desired results, instead of merely process completion.

Job Role—Focus on Results

Why focus on results? Very simply, skill development in generating results forms the substance of the promise to your people when they sign on with your company. Their career development is based upon growing their skills. This training is only meaningful if it supports people in their ability to generate results that the clients pay for.

If you have a new salesperson, your commitment to their training is to teach them enhanced sales, customer service, and account management skills. You never promised—nor did your employees join thinking—you would train them on their golf swing, even if they took clients out for the odd game of golf. However, I did witness a business development expert talk her boss into paying for her golf lessons. What can I say? Some people are great at sales.

The training is all designed to support them in growing their ability to generate results at a whole new level. That will propel the desired client results, and concurrently, the employees' careers.

An Example of Process versus Results in the Job Role

With a written job role, the question to consider is whether the areas of accountability are written as activities or results. How they are written will have a large impact on whether you are able to create a results-driven organization.

For example, you could say,

> "Provide and deliver safety training to our employees."

Or you could say,

> "Ensure the employees are trained and supported sufficiently to deliver their desired levels of client results in a safe and productive manner."

The first option is an activity you hope will generate the desired client result. The second one focuses on the desired result directly, leaving the employee the latitude to vary activities as needed to accomplish the desired result.

Training is part of both options. While the first option may ensure safety training compliance, what if employees also need coaching or mentoring to deliver results safely and in compliance with regulations?

Too often the issue occurs where a trainer completes delivery of the training, fully satisfying their job. Yet they didn't facilitate client results the staff training was designed to generate.

Further, the trainer doesn't have access to ensure they achieve the results without stepping beyond the scope of their written accountability. This constrains them. Clearly, the limitation is less than ideal for everyone.

By giving employees—in this case the trainer—a mandate that is focused on ensuring they achieve the desired result, they have a chance to do what it takes to win. They also get to own their job, rather than just being a cog in a larger system without access to their own direct accountability.

If you build both the purpose and each of the areas of accountability (the job chunks) with a focus on results, you will give your people cleaner access to their own sense of ownership of their roles. The wins they achieve will be theirs to enjoy, further supporting their growth.

The Growth Plan

While employees understand job requirements exist, they often still ask, "What about me? What do I get, other than the money?"

This is where the growth plan comes in.

This plan, initiated and fostered with each individual on every team, helps them see and co-create their growth and development over a three-to ten-year timeframe.

The plan is not just created once and left alone. Smart managers and team leaders quietly work with the plan through regular dialogue—at minimum quarterly check-ins—while weaving discussions about growth into their daily, weekly, and monthly work with team members.

Formulating a Career Development Growth Plan

I developed and refined ten questions over the past several years. Our team has successfully used this framework with company owners, senior managers, and employees to help generate effective growth plans for each staff person within the company.

The following questions lead to supporting someone to formulate their career development growth plan over the next decade. Each question is carefully crafted to support a productive flow of thinking. Together these questions lay the foundation for a stronger experience of professional growth within a company.

They also support you and your managers in getting to know your people at a whole new level.

In a dedicated session, the manager asks an employee each of these questions and takes notes as the person responds. Then they give the employee a copy of the notes while keeping a copy as well for their mutual use. Both people then work with the information within this document as the basis of encouraging the employee's continued professional growth.

Note: The method of achieving the learning outcomes (in question ten, below) will be accomplished through the implementation of the different aspects of their job, as outlined in the job role.

The Questions:

1. What are the job activities that give you energy?

Everyone has tasks or areas of work they enjoy more than others. These areas give the person energy. It is not only important to a manager to understand what feeds each employee's energy but also immensely helpful for the employees to notice this as well. Almost everyone will know this intuitively. Being able to express it helps crystallize these energizing areas for both manager and employee.

2. What job activities drain you?

While each person has tasks or areas of work they enjoy more than others, they also have areas that drain them. The rest are okay, neither feeding their energy nor sucking the life out of them. It is helpful to learn and understand which job activities fall into one of the two extremes for each of your people. That way, you and your managers can support them in tapping and growing their strengths. Where possible, you can also help them avoid the tasks that leave them feeling drained and miserable.

Everyone does so much better when using and growing the skills that align with their interests and energy.

Note: One important detail in this question is to specifically ask "What *job activities* drain you?" If you just ask, "What drains you?" without specifying "job activities," eight out of ten people answer with some version of "conflict." While that is useful to know, it doesn't give you access to which job activities are worse than others for the person.

3. What is your Superpower (biggest strength you like using that contributes to others)?

Everyone has one or more skills they love to contribute, generating activities they feel make a bigger difference to others than the rest of what they bring. This question provides an employee an opportunity to acknowledge this and share it with the manager.

Sometimes people are not clear on their superpower. If the person is not sure what you mean, you might ask, "What is the strongest skill or talent you have that gives you energy and makes a big, positive difference to others?"

If the person still has difficulty, the managers can share their perspective on what specifically they appreciate about the person's contribution.

4. What is your Kryptonite (biggest weak spot)?

Even Superman had a weakness, his "kryptonite." This gives your people permission to admit areas where they struggle. This perception from an employee is good information for the manager to know. When it is feasible for you to navigate the work to keep these activities away from the employee, their lives tend to be much brighter. Even if they need to learn something, bringing this subject up allows you to gain a clearer understanding of the employee, which you may not have had before.

Questions 4 and 5 also let the manager have a further glimpse into how self-aware the employee is about their own strengths and weak spots as well as what they would like to contribute. Understanding this is helpful to support people's growth and development. You want to support them in growing their strengths without falling into the trap of needing to grow their weaknesses where possible. That's what other team members—those with complementary strengths—are for.

5. What things help with the job (e.g. environment, tools, resources, processes, people, relationships, equipment)?

These items make a big difference to the quality of people's lives. The more you know about what makes life easier for them, the better equipped you will be with the information to continue to improve the conditions of their life at work. The items listed here are structures that support the employee to bring their best.

6. What things make the job harder?

This question can be construed as the opposite of question 5. However, I want to know if something—like conflict—is also having a negative impact on people. By placing this question right after 5, those who are aware of disruptive tools, environmental conditions, processes, or relationships have the chance to express this. However, if certain conflicts are present at work, they will inevitably arise when the question is left open, as it is here, without listing specific examples. This question may also give you a glimpse of either structures missing or impediments to supporting the employee to bring their best.

7. What are your favorite aspects of the role—things you enjoy, where you add the most value?

This links "favorite aspects" with things the person enjoys, which also add the most value. Never skip the value part. This whole conversation is about their growth at work, with their expertise, and toward the future they desire. Gaining their perspective on what they enjoy doing that also brings value is critical for managers. It also creates a link to productivity at work, quietly reinforcing a results orientation.

Before adding the "where you add the most value" part of the question, I would get back answers that included staff luncheons, summer BBQs, and other social activities over half the time.

8. In light of all this, what are your aspirations for the future? In other words, what you would like to be doing / contributing as you grow in your career?

The link between aspirations for the future and contribution is also intentional. You want to work with people who want to contribute. You are hiring for it. Support this notion at every turn. Part of the reason they are with you is because they also want to contribute. By formally linking these two notions, responses are much stronger and centered around giving to others. This is part of what supports people to thrive.

9. If you were to think of yourself in the future, ten years from now, what would you want to be able to say you achieved in your career over this next decade to have successful growth, both personally and professionally?

The purpose of this question is to support the employee in thinking about their future. Really encourage them to explore possibilities that are in line with where they see their career heading. How would they like to see themselves grow? What would success in their career look like? This is their chance to think *big*!

If they lack professional clarity, their personal aspirations might provide an entry point. These can help them dream of a brighter future based on what they enjoy creating or achieving.

Explore the question with them, and allow them time to think. This may be new territory for them to consider.

The key here is to encourage free thinking—dreaming really. The bigger they dream about their possible future, the more productive the next question will be.

10. What skills, experiences, and/or perspectives do you think you will you need to learn, develop, or refine over the next three years as a foundation to achieve your ten-year levels of progress on your career development journey?

This question, in most cases, is the most important in the series. Many of the others act as a pre-frame for this area of inquiry. This is your chance to co-create a path of learning and growth for your employee's development.

Let's say an employee wants to be president (or a senior executive) of the company in the next ten years, which comes up more often than you would think. What skills would this person need to learn over the next three years to be on track to achieve that position within ten years?

I recommend in this particular question, you or your manager dig in with the employee. When the employee gets stuck, suggest possible skills they may need that would support their progress in achieving the bigger future for themselves they seek.

Most people aren't sure what skills they may need to develop to attain and excel in a much higher level within the organization. If done well, the person's desired learning path will always be larger than their current role. This is exactly what you want.

One of the goals of this plan is to involve skill development beyond their current role. People should be learning at a level beyond while including what their current job entails. This piece is critical.

People often need help to identify specific skills they might need over the next three years to lay a strong foundation for the next decade. Too often, they think smaller than their future picture. After all, they have not been in those larger roles before. This is where the experience of the manager, or you as the owner, comes into the picture.

With experience as an aid, bosses can help provide guidance to employees on what they might want, or need, to learn to achieve their goals for career and professional growth as well as impact. To assist in this effort is totally appropriate. This is the one question of the ten where the participant may need some help.

A collaboration on brainstorming is appropriate as long as you don't start telling them what they need. By non-assertively asking questions that suggest possible skills they might consider necessary and letting them accept or decline those ideas, the plan remains theirs rather than feeling like something you built and assigned to them.

Other Observations

If you ask these questions with genuine interest and acknowledge the answers with real appreciation, the bond between you and your employee grows.

You are giving them the gift of your time and your attention. If authentically given, the relationship grows.

This process is not one to leave with people to fill out and return, even if you plan to discuss the topics later, at least not the first time through. One hundred percent of the time when initially digging into these areas, this meeting needs to be treated as very important, having your (or your manager's) attention. Otherwise, you'll lose the chance for trust building if you leave people to complete the questions on their own.

In fact, more often than not, when I have seen people hand these questions out in advance, the responses shift to what the employee thinks their boss wants to hear, which blocks and diminishes trust, rather than nurturing and enhancing the connection.

Overlaying the Growth Plan onto the Job Role

If this process is done properly, the things an employee needs to learn over a three-year period will be larger than the particular role they have at the moment.

The next step is simply to overlay the growth plan over the job role. The mechanisms to achieve the desired learning come from the job. Then, moving forward, the boss doesn't need to focus on the job itself. With the job and the growth plan overlaid, focusing on the growth plan achieves the job's goals while concurrently supporting the individual's career development.

If I regularly focus on a person's three-year learning objectives, using the project work as the mechanism of growth—which they have set with my assistance—we are prioritizing their growth agenda, not just my agenda for their current job, even as they complete the project work. This approach incorporates the job at hand, as success in achieving the three to five results outlined in the job role serves as a mutual measure of progress in both the growth plan and the client projects.

The two agendas become one. This is the only way it works. Unless the job role and the growth plan are integrated, a manager will not have enough time to properly address both. Then the growth plan will go to the wayside, as the job is what pays.

Either you, as owner, or one of your managers will be assisting your employees to achieve their goals for their career development, using the job role components and results to achieve this learning. Together with your employees, you keep the focus on them and the client concurrently, with no competition between the two objectives arising.

The employees continue to be served in their goals for growth. Employers get the job done while actively supporting the growth of the people, instead of treating them like cogs in some system they need to control.

Building Trust

Every single time I have worked with people to develop and institute growth plans within their company, the net effect is that trust builds between the employer and employee.

It's fascinating.

If you ask these questions authentically with the employees' true desires for their career growth as the only driving force, trust grows. No matter how strong the trust is already, employees at all levels appreciate the focus on what's important to them, rather than just focusing on what the leaders and managers of the company want.

This only endures and grows if their objectives are included and stay a part of the active dialogue between manager and employee consistently over time.

With a one-time instance of this activity, or if the process happens in any way other than through a live conversation, the opposite occurs. Trust can actually diminish.

Where This Can Go Wrong

If mishandled, this approach can go wrong very fast. I have seen people hand the questions to their employees to complete and return to the boss in advance of a meeting out of some desire for efficiency.

This is a crucial and costly mistake.

You do not build trust, which is the biggest thing you are after, along with increased connection through active and attentive communication regarding something very important to your people. The process is not just about the answers to the questions. Primarily, it is about treating people as valued members of the team and ensuring they feel it. Only then do the questions and their answers matter.

The real gift is your time and attention, but only if accompanied with authentic interest.

If these questions are handed to employees in advance, they tend to fill them out in ways they think will impress the boss or with some other agenda in mind, rather than authentically sharing what is important to them. After all, they think, If I get it right, I may be able to accelerate my raise or promotion.

The purpose of impressing the boss can't be the driver of this discussion. The process only has a chance if you take the time to ask and listen in a way that shows your genuine interest in your employee's development within the firm. Otherwise, you are back to the 20th-century boss as the source of power, and the employee reverts to being the cog in the system.

People want to feel seen, and they want to feel heard for who they really are. Only by granting those most valuable resources to them—your time and your attention without rushing them— can they build trust in you and in the partnership you are forming.

A Further Caution

I saw one instance of this where the boss worked with the employee on the first few questions. Then they ran out of time, so the boss asked the employee to fill in the rest, so they could circle back to review it together the next day. The trust they'd built in the first meeting was lost. Even the boss noticed the shift when the two subsequently got together. It took two more meetings to reestablish this bond with the employee.

"Our trust is strong. It should be okay." I also hear this.

Yes, your trust may be strong, but this is a very specific exercise to bond two people further together based upon what is important to the employee. This is the only way to generate true partnerships and alliances. Don't blow it in the name of efficiency.

It is better not to do this at all rather than to try any of these shortcuts.

Done well, this can eliminate "Us-Them" in companies and actually have people bring their best, collaborate, and create magic. And yes, this does happen consistently.

The Reality of the Situation

You're paying this person anywhere from a low of about thirty thousand dollars (that's fifteen dollars per hour), to hundreds of thousands of dollars or more over the course of a year. What is the cost to you to take one or two meetings of a couple of hours each to understand and be able to work with what is truly important to someone who commits to help you grow your company? Once you've completed the growth plan questionnaire, it turns into a discussion and check-in point, not a whole multi-hour energy suck.[2]

By actively working with and overlaying the job role and the growth plan—two core pieces of an employee's participation in the company—the team members are each individually set up to generate their part of the desired results.

But what about the development of teams? That is coming next.

2. We'll touch more on how this can work when we talk about the development and growth of your managers and leaders, coming up in their own chapters.

11

FOCUS ON TEAMS

LET'S TALK ABOUT TEAMS.

If your people are key to gaining freedom, teams multiply that power. People working together in teams drive everything that is good in your company.

Without them, life gets a lot harder.

If your company has grown beyond the first danger zone, approaching two million in revenue, chances are good your people are pretty good at working with each other to get projects done. It used to be they would join your company to do a job. You put them into situations where they could do that job, and as their expertise grew, they became more effective over time.

Okay. That's no big deal. It's what you are used to doing.

Most people simply put two or three workers together on a project, call them a "team," and leave them to figure things out. But calling them a team doesn't make them one.

Soon enough, the cracks start to show up.

Biggest Issues

The biggest issues with teams usually come down to one of two areas:

1. Having the wrong people on the team, or
2. Struggling with team relationships and how to get people to work together effectively.

Problems that crop up on a team seem to be either a competence problem or a relationship problem.[1]

Competence: "I thought I had good people on this team, but they aren't delivering, so I must need more skilled or more senior people. My manager is trying hard, and she's sincere. She used to deliver when she was an individual producer. I must have the wrong people working for her."

Relationship: "The people on this team don't trust each other. Maybe we need to send them away for a relationship building program so they will work better together."

Hmm.

What if it is something else?

Like most things, there are the surface issues, and then there are the underlying issues that hide beneath the surface—the structural issues that impact the symptoms you can see.

---

1. Mark Samuel has done good work in this area. His 2021 book, **Reimagine Teams: The Missing Piece in Team Building to Achieve Breakthrough Results**, sheds light on how to improve teams and teamwork in meaningful ways. Some of the ideas which I have implemented with clients and I share here, come from his work in this area.

Most of the competence and relationship issues that arise have structural underpinnings.

In other words, the problem is usually this: The underlying structures needed to support effective teamwork haven't been addressed. Without these supportive structures, people either appear unqualified or end up in conflicts with each other. Often, the only structures present are those designed to corral or constrain behavior, which makes an already difficult situation worse.

What's the difference between a team and a collection of people? Many owners just haven't thought about this. They just label the collection as a team and get on with it.

Then they wonder why their teams don't work as well as they had hoped. Is this a trap you have fallen into? If so, you certainly are not alone.

People Haven't Been Trained for Teamwork

Think about it for a minute. In school you were always told to:

1. Work hard;
2. Make sure you complete what you start;
3. Do your own work;
4. Whatever you do, don't cheat!

In school, cheating meant relying on someone else to do the hard parts for you.

Building a Team Is a Design Issue

One of the goals of working in teams is to tap the power of complementary strengths of different people. If one of your people has an area of strength, he is expected to contribute that. Someone with a different complementary skill can bring that to the table. If people are going to rely on each other's strengths, they need to understand what those are and which are held by whom. The group also needs to be able to allow for the contributions of each member.

However, working together still goes against everything we have been taught throughout our careers. More than taught. This has been drilled into our brains and our habits since we were youngsters. The result is most people, owners included, are not as good at navigating through this new terrain. For you and your managers, that causes stress and reactive behavior.

What does it take to build an effective team? While a number of different factors are at play in team development, one of the most basic yet critical components in expertise-based teams is to expand your perspective on what you want to achieve.

In other words, set better goals.

Team Goals Expanded

There are four distinct sets of goals in project-based work.

1. **Achievement of Client Deliverables**—This is the one area that everyone knows and follows. Even with this, tightening up what constitutes a complete project, done by some but not all project managers, can make your deliverables stronger.

2. **Individual Learning/Growth of Team Members**—Since you now have growth plans for each member of the team, identify what skills or expertise each person wants to develop through project delivery. Adding this dimension of goals energizes people.

3. **Team Goals**—How do your people want to work with each other to generate the best possible results? Talking through people's respective superpowers and how they would like to contribute will accelerate your team and create stronger results for the project, for each individual, and also for the team.

4. **Company-Focused Results**—What are the company's goals from this project? There will be goals for gross profits achieved. Yet there may be more. For example, growth in reputation in a project type or industry, increase in internal capabilities, or use of the project to help streamline an internal process may be other potential goals that move the company forward.

Expanding the goals you set for your projects supports increased teamwork, more appreciation of each person's skills, and stronger team relationships, all while achieving real-time client results.

Teams as Structures for Company Growth

When companies are smaller, teams are a natural place to generate larger project results. What if this structure could be maintained and grown to support people's individual growth as well? Then competency frameworks won't be needed. Instead, you will be able to stick to what makes a difference to your clients—their project results.

You have individual teams of knowledge workers focused on generating results. What structure could complement this approach to help grow your people more directly?

Two Structural Supports

There are numerous ways to integrate additional structures to achieve both client results and individual growth. Here are two possibilities.

1. Project Teams and "Homerooms"—When I was in high school, my fellow students and I had many different classes with different teachers. However, every student also had a homeroom teacher who took attendance, monitored overall progress across all classes, and served as a consistent point of contact and support throughout the year. In business, this same structure can work effectively. A dedicated manager serves as the "homeroom," monitoring each team member's overall professional development and providing guidance, even as people move between different project teams. This system has proven successful with many clients.

2. Mentoring Programs—Another method we have successfully used has been individual mentoring of staff in addition to their project teams. Each person works directly with their project manager on client initiatives. Someone outside that team (one of the other managers) takes a certain number of people for one-on-one mentoring and support, encouraging their continued development in ongoing individual conversations.

The mentor also collaborates with project managers to track progress and measure successes and learnings from the different projects undertaken by each mentee. Even as projects and their leaders change, the individual employee has an enduring person there to support them through their growth.

This is similar to the homeroom notion but with an increased focus on each team member's professional growth, acting as a resource or sounding board where needed.

These are only two possible ways to keep teams at the heart of results-based growth of your people. Both of these systems have been successfully implemented many times across companies in a wide variety of industries.

With the evolution of a team-based structure, growth of people becomes more predictable for the company overall.

Of course, this also creates levels of stability that you will need within your organization as you grow, to gain increased freedom.

Summary

Many don't take the time to think through their teamwork with each other. Nor do they explore how teams may be used as part of an enduring structure that can facilitate professional growth.

Leaders who actively focus on how a team works enjoy life at work more. They are able to make a bigger difference with less effort, fewer problems, and more satisfaction.

These are important elements of an intelligent ecosystem. A strong ecosystem will assist you to gain increased freedom.

Another element of the ecosystem, and a key to freedom, is how you manage your people.

That's coming up next!

12

GROW MANAGERS

As early as danger zone 1, when you approach two million in revenue, you will start building out layers between you, the owner, and your teams. This is where management comes in.

The Conundrum of Management

One of the most misunderstood roles in a company is that of a manager. This role probably has more lingering issues from 20th-century Industrial Age practices than any other part of that era.

It may also be the hardest job in the company.

Often, managers have multiple bosses and multiple employees, each with constantly changing needs. Managers are consistently given more responsibility than authority, and they are expected to "make it work."

What Is Management?

One of the best functional definitions I have found came from Marcus Buckingham,[1] who was a senior leader with the Gallup organization before he started his own international research company to continue his studies on employees and management. He defined the role of management quite well.

Management*—to take the talents of people and turn them into performance.*

Unfortunately, just because we have a working definition of management doesn't mean that confusion in this segment of the business world is reduced. In fact, many different practices—from positive to manipulative or even destructive—have been established and used in the name of managers generating performance.

If management is about taking the talents of people and turning them into performance, why is there such disarray in middle management? Why do we get some bosses who are great and others who are horrible?

Doesn't this definition create a clear path to success in management?

Apparently not. Knowing what management is doesn't mean everyone will be good at it.

Best Boss/Worst Boss

Almost everyone in business has encountered, heard about, or been fortunate enough to work directly for a great boss. We have also

1. Marcus Buckingham has given many talks on this subject. His definitions of management and leadership are both practical and functionally useful. Further information from Buckingham may be found on his web site marcusbuckingham.com

either worked under, witnessed, or heard about bad bosses in companies as well.

What distinguishes the great bosses from their nightmare counterparts?

When delivering our management training program, one of the questions I ask participants to consider is this.

Best Boss

> "Who is the best boss you have worked for, and what made them the best?"

Here is a small sampling of some of the most common attributes groups come up with through this exercise:

- Shows integrity
- Communicates well
- Has a sense of fun
- Shows humility
- Knows their own strengths and limitations
- Shows compassion
- Displays charisma
- Maintains positivity
- Encourages self- development
- Stays approachable
- Provides support and inclusion
- Enables personal growth
- Listens actively
- Brings out the best in others

Worst Boss

I also ask people about the worst boss they have ever encountered and the list of attributes associated with these people. Here are a few of the more common responses.

- Unable to make a decision
- "My way or the highway"
- Shows no humanity
- Talks down to people
- Displays entitlement
- Acts dishonestly (zero integrity)
- Sets expectations without providing proper tools
- Refuses to listen or allow input
- Demonstrates poor follow-through
- Blocks others' contributions
- Shows no respect
- Acts self-absorbed
- Behaves dictatorially
- Doesn't listen or allow for others
- "Takes credit for my ideas"
- Treats others like objects

What is the Difference?

The best bosses see their job and their people differently.

They listen to their people, focusing on their strengths and what might make them better while fostering their growth. The worst ones, by contrast, seem to "drive over people" to get what they want or disregard them completely.

Prescribed Power versus Power of Influence

Another way to summarize the difference is to say that the worst bosses use prescribed power—the power granted from their position—to get their people to act.

The best bosses don't use their prescribed power. Instead, they use "power of influence." They gain influence by earning credibility with their people. They don't push themselves on anyone. They will stand up for what they believe in, but even then, they are working with the credibility and influence they have earned with their people. They don't expect anything by virtue of the title they hold.

This distinction is critical to understand the difference between 20th-century management, which is based almost entirely on prescribed power, and 21st century management, which is based on power of influence.

Your Team's Willingness to Work with a Manager

The next couple of questions I asked workshop participants yielded no surprises.

1. "What was your willingness to give your best for your best boss?"
2. "What about the worst one?"

"Best bosses" have more trust from, and better results generated with their people. With the "worst bosses," most participants just wanted to quit. And sure enough, eventually they did.

One question I ask in these workshops catches most participants by surprise.

"Do you really believe the bad bosses intended to be so horrible, or did they even know they were so bad?"

Most participants end up realizing that, with only a few exceptions, their bad bosses probably had no idea how awful they were to work for. These bosses were completely unconscious to their impact on many of the people who work for them. Participants also decided that perhaps a few bad bosses knew they weren't any good at being the boss, but they didn't know how to change it.

In fact, the statistics bear this out. In surveys of over 150,000 managers and over one million employees, Gallup found that 71 percent of all managers ranked themselves in the top 20 percent of all managers.[2]

Hang on.

71 percent of all managers rank themselves in the top 20 percent of all managers?

Yes.

In other words, your managers have no idea if they are any good as managers or not. But most think they do know, and think they are good at it. This statistic starts to wake people up to the realization that things may not be as rosy as they think.

Hmm.

What's the Problem?

The fundamental problem is that most managers, raised with the

---

2. Many of these surveys were conducted from 1977 through 1997 and first published in First Break All the Rules, What the World's Greatest Managers Do Differently, by Marcus Buckingham and Curt Coffman, © 1999 Gallup Inc. More information and the latest survey results on this subject may be found on the website, www.gallup.com.

20th-century mentality, think they need to control their people in order to get the best from them.

They may have the wrong people on the team. Or possibly they know how to do the job, so they decide they just need to tell these more junior people how to do it.

They also may feel the responsibility of standing accountable for the collective results of the whole team when they have previously been accountable for their own results.

The Core Issue

The fundamental issue is that managers typically get promoted to this position due to their accomplishments of doing the work needed in their former job as an individual contributor.

As individual workers, they learned their role and excelled in it. Their skills and knowledge both grew over time, sometimes taking years to become experts in their craft. Yet the skills needed to manage other people in the 21st century are pretty much the opposite of the skills needed to do the job as an individual contributor.

Background

To understand where you and your managers stub your toes (*ouch!*) regarding the notion of management, we need to first start with what happens when new employees join the workforce.

When you got your first post-school, full-time job, you needed to learn how to master that role. In a trade or profession driven by the expertise of the people, this may have taken many years. Several different levels of mastery are required to become accomplished within most fields of expertise.

At all times, there is the thinking to master. This can be multilayered as well. Often, especially within skilled trades, and also in different parts of the health care field, physical skills are also involved. A surgeon better learn how to use a scalpel well.

Regardless of the field or area of expertise, the goal is to learn how to generate results that matter to your clients and customers. After all, that is what clients and customers pay for.

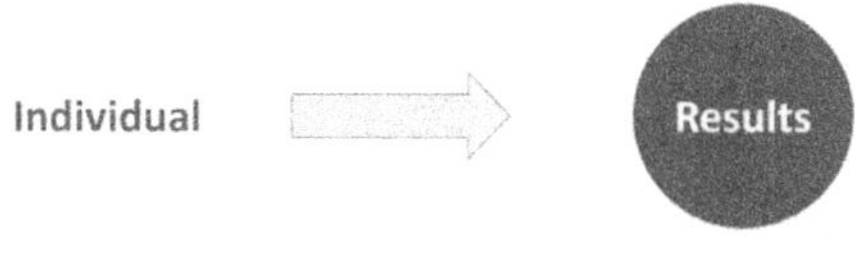

Figure 12.1

When you were a new employee, your job was to perform the tasks needed to achieve the desired results. You developed the skills and habits to do this consistently over time, to stronger and deeper levels. This increased your value as an employee.

How do people become bosses in the first place? You as the owner, are impressed with their work ethic, their ability to generate results, and their use of good judgment along the way. Clearly, they would make the best choice to move into management.

"No one knows the elements of making things work like Max. I trust him completely. He does the job well and treats our customers with care and understanding. He should lead that team!"

Becoming a Great Boss

How does someone learn how to be a great boss? The short answer is: usually, they don't. They either bring a natural aptitude for it or a small few stumble into effective practices over time.

Yet, most people assume they know how to manage.

"How hard can it be? I know the job really well, and I know how to talk to people. I just need to show others how to do what I do and we will be all set."

If you don't know that you don't know, you assume you know.

This has almost universally disastrous consequences on most people who enter management.

The habits people have developed to generate direct technical results have become embedded. Since they have learned to rely on these habitual skills, they are hard-pressed to let these go, especially when these skills have served them so well in delivering individual results. There's only one problem with this. The habits you have established as an individual contributor actually get in the way of being effective as a manager.

For Instance

As an individual contributor, you need to develop knowledge, skills, and a way to think your way through issues. You either share conclusions, or use them to generate results. Yet as a manager, that's not your job. As a manager, you need to support people to grow their skills at thinking through complex issues. Telling people answers blocks their ability to evolve their own thinking. What you tell them are your thoughts, not theirs. If you tell them, they don't have a chance to develop their own thinking.

The fact is, most people in professions and trades take pride in their work. They feel satisfaction in their growth within their field or discipline, and their ability to accomplish more as they learn more. This is tied to their technical skills development and either a solutions focus or a customer-centric focus.

We think of managers as accountable for the results of their whole team. This is what it looks like.

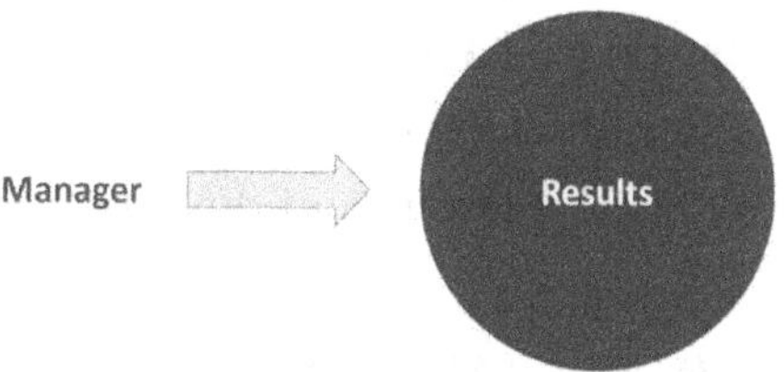

Figure 12.2

Business owners want their people to be accountable for results. When performance lags or becomes inconsistent, they expect managers to hold staff accountable.

If you apply 21st century thinking, this model is just inaccurate. It also doesn't work very well, except for the most short-term results.

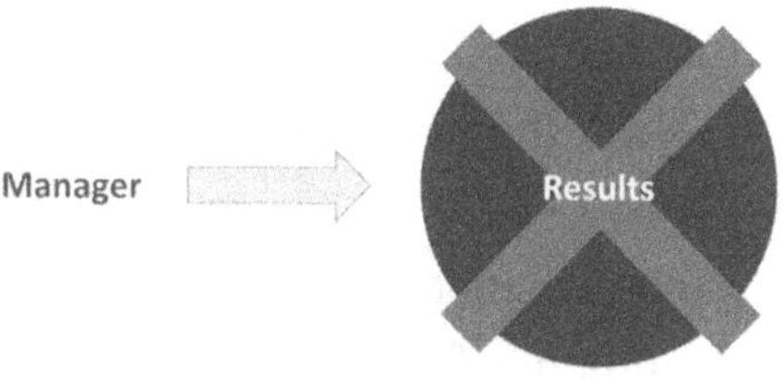

Figure 12.3

The thinking has some 20th century flaws in it. Two related flaws come to mind.

1. **First of all, there is no such thing as "holding someone else accountable,"** despite how often this phrase appears in business and elsewhere. And let's not kid ourselves—it is used constantly!
    - The very notion of "holding someone else accountable" implies a level of control that managers simply don't have. Attempting to exert such control is silly. While this approach was common in the 20th-century Industrial Age, in the

21st century, we have a term for this—bullying. That is literally what created the need for unions in business back at the turn of the 20th century.

2. **Alternatively, employees leave accountability to their manager.** If a manger is responsible for the bigger result, employees think they no longer are.
   - Even if it could be argued that this is technically correct (you need to adopt "command and control" management thinking to do that), it doesn't make room for employee ownership of results. "If the manager is accountable, I must not be."
   - Employees who want accountability will feel robbed of the opportunity to step into the role and excel at it. The credit invariably goes to the person accountable… the manager.

On the other hand, when the team members are individually and collectively accountable for the whole result, the manager is only accountable for the whole result as a member of that team, just like each other person on the team, not instead of them.

This is the 21st century reality.

Stop Telling People What to Do

People who excel enough to become managers typically do more than just follow directions. They think independently and generate superior results by bringing their own insights to their work. This is precisely why simply telling people what to do creates several problems.

1. **If you tell me something, I feel "told."** This quietly conveys that I am somehow "less than" the person who

is telling me (you in this case). Even if I know that you know more than me, I might resist since I had no part in thinking it through.

2. **Even if I just accept what you tell me, and it generates a win, I attribute that win to you rather than owning it myself.** After all, it was your idea. I feel a bit like the underling or, said differently, a cog in a larger system rather than an active and valued partner in it. In a services business, being robbed of my ability to think is not a good thing.

3. **If I really don't like being told what to do, I will "check out."** Sure, I may put up with it for a while, mentally checking out, doing what you say, and taking your money, especially if the pay is good. Eventually, even this gets old, so I start actively looking for another job, where I have a chance to contribute and not merely operate as your follower, or "set of hands" without a brain.

Under this arrangement, people are separate from the core of the business, not part of it, as indicated in chapter 7—Rethink the Core.

Individual contributors have one primary job—generating results. That's what they learned how to do, and they became good at it.

This holds true for all employees who deliver results, including those who haven't been promoted to management. Their job, specifically, is to generate the same kinds of results their managers once delivered when they held similar positions.

If that is the case, what is the job of their manager? Back to this question… again? *Ugh!*

Support Them in Their Accountability

The job of a manager is to support people in their individual and collective accountabilities. In other words, to help the growth of the people who generate the results. This help, as long as it isn't taking over, doesn't rob people of their own accountability.

Instead of "holding people accountable," the manager holds people "*as accountable*," and partners with them in that accountability. Though subtle, this is entirely different from holding others accountable (i.e., attempting to control them, to get them to do what you want).

Supporting others in their accountability allows your people to remain accountable. Further, it contributes to them in a meaningful way.

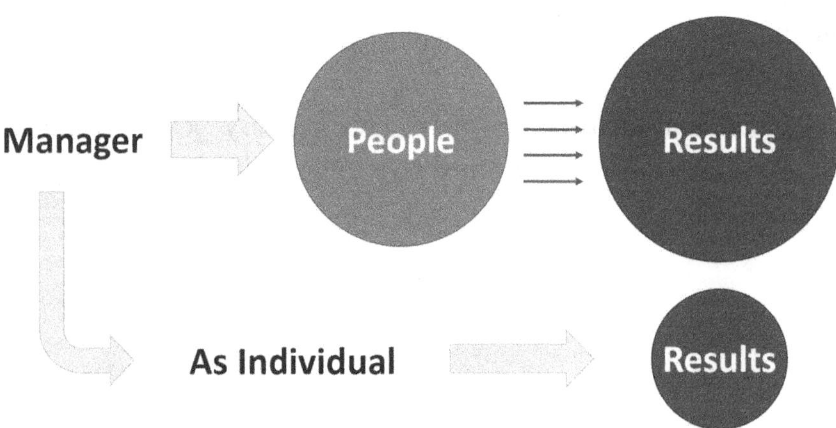

Figure 12.4

The Job

Managers need to:

1. Get to know their people to the point of understanding what makes them tick. This means learning their strengths (to tap), weaknesses (to avoid), and how they prefer to work with others. Beyond clarifying individual roles, managers must show how these roles interconnect to generate collective results.

2. Support individual growth based on understanding each team member. The career development growth plans, based in developing their thinking, and overlaid onto the person's job role, are critical to success here.

3. Grow the team and support employees in the skills and habits needed to effectively work together to generate the collective outcomes, not just individual results. This is why number 2 in the Social Contract is so important.
4. Nurture the evolution of the company's culture within the team. This is an extension of number 3 but deserves separate attention. A strong culture supports people's growth, development, and ability to generate individual and collective results.

Owner/Company	Individual Employees
1. Generate individual client results	1. Compensation
2. Work together to generate collective client results	**2. Professional training and growth**
3. Develop a stronger corporate culture	3. Access to meaningful work
4. Progress toward the company's larger purpose	4. Access to developing meaningful relationships

Management is a bigger job than most people realize. No wonder it proves so challenging!

How Many People to Manage?

One question that I hear constantly is, "What is the right number of people for a manager to manage?"

The right number of people to manage is the number of people a manager can consistently meet with, one-to-one, each and every week. If that is only two people, due to that manager's individual workload, then two is the right number. If a manager has been freed up from their own individual deliverables and can meet with eight people per week—one-to-one—then eight is the right number for that person.

Why One-To-One?

If you accept that a manager's job is to support the people, who in turn generate the results, the answer to this is simple. People need support in real time. That means at least weekly. Getting it every two to three weeks is not helpful.

The statistics bear this out. Numerous studies indicate that a weekly one-on-one meeting with a manager generates an average of 13 percent increase in productivity of the employee. However, holding a one-on-one meeting every three weeks has a *5 percent reduction in productivity!*

Not meeting at all has a higher productivity than meeting less often than weekly. Weekly meetings support the actual work the person is doing, in real time. Anything less frequent, even every other week, loses this specific benefit of "real-time support" and feels like "the boss is checking up on me."

Group meetings (or team huddles) don't make up for this. It needs to be one-on-one, and it needs to be every week.

I'm not talking about an hour meeting every week. Not even a half hour.

It could be as short as a ten-to-fifteen-minute weekly meeting to check in to see how things are going and what support the person might need. Even if the employee consistently says things are fine and they don't need further support, these meetings are crucial and have a positive impact.

Feelings of support aside, the meetings also give the manager the pulse on the team: who is doing well and who might be having difficulties, either at work or home, that may be weighing on the person's mind. Small issues are much easier to address when caught early rather than leaving them to grow while people feel stuck about how to handle them. That is part of what support is all about.

Growth of Managers

Between the client relationships, the project work, and the needs of their people, it is no surprise that what appear to be less important (okay, less urgent) matters seem to slip through the cracks. Even when management training is provided, some—though fewer—problems continue. Life seems to get more complex as the organization grows.

To grow into their constantly evolving roles, managers need ongoing support too.

Enter the leaders.

13

DEVELOP LEADERS

EFFECTIVE LEADERSHIP IS A CRITICAL ELEMENT IN ECOSYSTEM development and in gaining increased freedom in, from, and because of your business.

So much has been written about leadership that I initially hesitated to write this chapter.[1] Of course, when a lot is written about a subject, there tends to be inconsistency in what is offered.

So, instead, I am going to address things that most don't.

Leadership: The Myths and Misconceptions

The most common things I see in business publications are endless lists of attributes that somebody needs to have to be a great leader.

---

1. A number of great authors have written one or more books on leadership. Here are some I like and follow: The Arbinger Institute, *Leadership and Self-Deception*; Jeb Blount, *People Follow You*; Marcus Buckingham, *The One Thing You Need to Know* and *Nine Lies About Work*; Kevin Cashman, *Leadership From the Inside Out*; Jim Collins, his whole series of books—*Built to Last*, *Good to Great*, *Great by Choice*, *How the Mighty Fall*, *BE 2.0*; Daniel Goleman, *Primal Leadership*; Henry Kissinger, *Leadership*; Patrick Lencioni, *The Five Dysfunctions of a Team* and all his other books on teams and leadership; Jo Owen, *How to Lead*.

To me, this is a great example of the—*dreaded?*—competency framework, only applied to leadership. While those lists sound truly noble, I have yet to meet one person who meets them all, or even comes close, even though I've met many great leaders in business.

Leaders only have one thing in common—followers. That's it.

For some reason (and the reasons are all different), people choose to follow a leader. The key word is "choose." They don't follow because they must. They do so from their own choice.

A useful functional definition of leadership, again from Marcus Buckingham, is "*to rally people to a brighter future*."

This aligns with the notion that our perceived future shapes our present. If we see a brighter future, we are happier, and more productive in the present.

When Leaders Are Needed... Beyond the Owner

Once the company grows beyond a certain level—which varies wildly from company to company, and even in some cases department by department—there is a need for what feels like an extra layer between the owner(s) and managers. This is where the company's top leaders come in.

Disparity of Leaders—An Example

I worked with a company that developed and operated remote work camps in northern Canada, providing accommodation and services for resource industry workers. These camps ranged from small facilities housing forty to sixty workers to large operations with four hundred to six hundred people, each running for two-to three-year contracts.

The operational side was substantial, with departments for food services, housekeeping, and facilities maintenance, plus a construction division that built and dismantled the camps. A VP of Operations oversaw well over one hundred people through a structure of area managers who supported individual site managers.

By contrast, the sales team consisted of just three people, despite revenue in the tens of millions per year. Since each contract was large, they didn't need many salespeople. The VP of Sales directly managed this small team. Similarly, the finance team had only six people under the CFO.

So we had three senior leaders with vastly different scopes: a VP of Operations accountable for over one hundred people, a CFO managing six people, and a VP of Sales leading three people. The skills needed differed greatly among these groups, and rightly so. To make sweeping statements about what leaders "need to be" (read competencies) is so common that we don't notice it. Yet we don't all have—or even need—the same skills, even on different teams in the same company. It is far more productive to look at leadership from a results perspective.

Fundamentally, other than access to the senior leaders' table, the CFO and VP of Sales were both high-level managers. So let's start by revisiting the role of the manager.

The Job of Managers Summarized

A manager's job is to support their people in turning their talents into collective performance that delivers measurable value to clients at the company's targeted profit levels. They do this as part of the core of the company.

Managers support their people through:

1. Building teams of knowledge workers with complementary strengths

2. Supporting these teams to work together to achieve desired results
3. Fostering their professional growth, both as individuals and as teams That's a pretty tall order.

How do leaders fit into this?

The Role of Leaders

The teams within an organization are accountable for their individual and collective results. The managers are accountable for those results as well, in their capacity as a fully functioning member of their team, just like the other team members.

This holds true for the leaders too. Leaders are accountable for the results in their respective areas as parts of the teams that include the team members and their managers. In fact, a leader's team may well be a group of managers, who each support their respective teams and team members.

The role of leaders might look something like this.

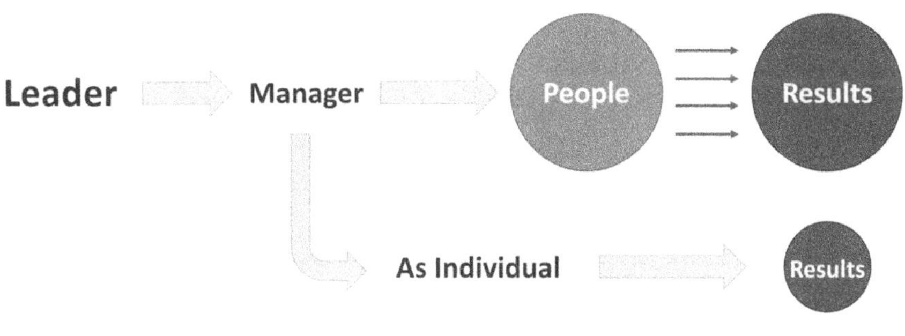

Figure 13.1

To break down the areas of accountability for leaders within services firms where expertise plays a major role—knowing these would vary somewhat from company to company—the areas of accountability might look like this.

Leaders: Areas of Responsibility

1. Co-create and unfold a compelling future
2. Build and strengthen the corporate culture
3. Support managers in developing their teams and team members
4. Develop and grow existing and future leaders

If a company adopts these areas of responsibility, even leaders of small teams may be seconded to support other managers within the organization, as they grow in their leadership journey.

As mentioned above, much has been written on leadership, and numbers 1 and 2 above have been covered well in many other books.

The areas that don't seem to get enough attention are numbers 3 and 4—supporting managers and developing existing and future leaders.

3. Support Managers in Developing Their Teams and Team Members

One of the key responsibilities for leaders is to support the managers in developing their teams sufficiently to allow them to achieve the goals for project and company deliverables.

This is where things get interesting. With clarity on the goals of client projects, goals for the growth and development of their teams, and career pathways for each individual, managers have the tools to support their people to build powerful teams. Yet it doesn't usually go that way. Life has a funny habit of intervening to spoil our plans.

Managers need solid and ongoing support to achieve these

objectives. Without active support, especially junior managers get swallowed up by all the noise in their projects.

The environment is constantly shifting. That means people—think team members—are in a constant state of adapting to the changes.

Or are they?

Habits

Our ability as humans to develop habits allows us to free our conscious bandwidth to focus on the changes as they occur. We need stable routines we can count on or we risk losing our way. This applies to managers as well. They developed certain habits when they were directly responsible for client deliverables—responsibilities some may still retain as part of their team duties.

The very habits that served them well as individual contributors can now hinder their effectiveness as managers. While these established patterns helped them succeed before, they often clash with the demands of management.

These exact habits will drive managers to tell people what to do rather than listen to their team's input—defaulting to their own established ways of operating based on their previous direct experiences.

Managers, especially new managers, fall into the trap of micromanaging their people, though with honest intentions. But that doesn't mean micromanagement has a place in their new role.

That's where you, as their leader, come into the picture.

With the constant changes occurring, affecting your teams and your client projects, client deliverables are perpetually shifting.

Habits your managers developed for their benefit when they were only practitioners were incredibly useful to them. Now they just get in the way of the real job—supporting their people to develop their own habits while helping them grow the ability to think through increasingly complex situations that come with project work.

Any questions why we need solid leaders to support our managers?

4. Develop the Leadership Skills of Managers

The future of the company lies in the growth of its people, perhaps even more than in its strategy. That spans from front-line knowledge workers to support staff, from production teams to sales teams. This also extends to the managers who support them along the way.

What about the leaders? They need to be supported in their growth as well, often rising through the ranks of the organization.

Risks of Bringing in Outsiders

I have seen a number of instances where senior people are brought in from outside the firm, presumably to lead the company to the next levels of growth and prosperity.

There are pros and cons with this approach.

Business Owners are frequently left with the situation where the company has grown faster than it could upskill its internal people, leaving a gap that can only be filled from outside the company's walls. "We don't have anyone who can lead us right now. We need to bring in someone from the outside."

On the plus side, we may find someone who has the skills and experience to lead us to the next level. This can be quite helpful, even transformational.

However, at senior leadership levels, new hires inevitably bring their own cultural perspectives that differ from the existing company culture. This move can cause unexpected terrible side effects, such as transforming your way out of your current culture.

It becomes a bigger risk, the higher the position in the company you fill.

To manage that risk and its unfortunate consequences, many take a more controlled approach and bring someone into the lower level of leadership or the upper end of management, instead of going higher. This allows for time to acclimate the person to the company's culture before the person grows into a higher position within the company.

Developing Leaders: What It Takes

Growing future managers and leaders may seem daunting, but it usually takes less than you fear. While this process requires shifts in thinking, these changes can be accomplished by supporting the growth of people over time.

The Shifts from Manager to Leader

Leaders do their best work when they grow leadership skills and leadership perspectives in their managers. Managers need to learn how to do three things:

1. Master management skills,
2. Adopt three key perspectives, and
3. Support independent thinking.

1. Master Management Skills

Leaders need to support managers in mastering all the skills that were listed in the management chapter. The key shift is moving from hands-on execution to supportive guidance, helping others achieve their client goals rather than prescribing specific methods.

Leaders, armed with a bit of distance from the day-to-day aspects of the business, are in the best position to provide managers with the ongoing support they need to develop these skills.

2. Adopt Three Key Perspectives

The biggest thing leaders can contribute to managers and others who are growing as future leaders is to model and provide access to three key perspectives. With these perspectives, combined with the ability to operate in their management roles, managers can grow into effective leaders.

The three key perspectives needed to shift from manager to leader are:

1. Look from a higher altitude and a longer view,
2. Show genuine care for people's growth and prosperity, and
3. Trust people in teams to figure things out.

Perspective 1: A Higher Altitude and Longer View

There is a phrase, "caught in the weeds." It refers to dealing with the micro details at ground level. If I am looking at a two-foot by three-foot garden, I can see all the weeds. If I were to focus on the weeds within a full one-acre parcel of land, the whole thing would feel overwhelming.

When I look at the same property from one hundred feet in the air—let's say from a helicopter—I don't see the weeds at all, in either the garden or the larger parcel of land. I only see the plots of land themselves at that altitude and where they sit relative to the house on that property. The details of the smaller garden aren't visible, but the colors of the larger field are visible.

As I go higher, to about five hundred feet, the colors of the larger field aren't as well- defined. However, the house and property are contrasted against the other properties in the area. More pronounced are the rivers, lakes and forests in the area.

If I go up even further, to one thousand feet, I see the subdivision of homes and the surrounding landscape. I can start to see what's off in the distance—the topography overall.

Each altitude has its own view, yielding a different perspective.

When managers get stuck, they are typically stuck in a low altitude view. They seem to have too much to process and too many disparate, moving parts to navigate to get the job done well.

Of course, the development of the people on the team is a longer-range endeavor, requiring a higher altitude and patience to allow skills to evolve and good judgment to mature. When people push for an answer too soon, from an immediate need, those people tend to get stuck.

A leader can give a manager that longer-range view. This is another dimension of a higher altitude. In many cases the urgency of the immediate need tends to dissipate with the longer-term perspective.

One of the most important things a leader can provide a manager is access to that higher altitude and that longer-term view. This gives the manager room to breathe without the immediacy of the urgent pressing in.

Perspective 2: Show Genuine Care for People's Growth and Prosperity

What was the difference between the companies that worked through the danger zones versus the ones who got stuck?

It all came down to the care and consideration they had for their people.

When the owners, and by extension the top leaders genuinely cared about their people, putting them first over systems and structures, they were able to more effectively scale the hurdles. They still had to hold clear boundaries of who fit into their organization and who shouldn't be there.

Those who put up with everyone, claiming to care for their people, got stuck, usually in danger zone 2 or 3. These companies would vacillate between certain revenue levels with lower profits than they wanted, plagued by ongoing people problems.

If a leader can work with managers on one thing, it is to live from this care and commitment to the people and their well-being. There is a big difference between talking about caring for people and living from a true commitment to care for them. People who put their teams first don't talk about it. This thinking is a core part of the basis for all their decisions and actions.

Managers need to feel this perspective and be allowed to have it grow into their thinking on an ongoing basis. Leaders who think from the "people-first" perspective can't help but have it become part of their guidance of the managers they support.

Perspective 3: Trust People in Teams to Figure Things Out

If you have hired smart people and are building your teams based in complementary strengths, the biggest thing you can do as a leader is get out of the way and allow your people to do their thing. Advanced leaders know this. They need to support their managers to operate this way as well.

This is difficult for managers, who are still breaking the habits of being expert "doers" to generate their own results. The smartest of them are trying to break the habit of "doing" to allow others to do, and instead guiding their growth together.

Managers will get in the way of their people. They need to learn to trust their people, operating in teams, to figure things out. This is one of the best lessons you as a leader can instill in your managers who are growing into leadership positions themselves.

This requires managers to stop telling people what to do. This will likely be the hardest lesson managers will face. However, it is vital to their success as managers and critical if they want to develop as leaders.

The only thing worse than managers who hold on to "telling" are leaders who do the same.

3. Support Independent Thinking

The natural inclination of managers, and anyone who has developed levels of expertise is to share what they know (telling). The skill of avoiding advice-giving and replacing it with observations and questions doesn't come naturally.

It comes with wisdom.

If you tell me what to do, I do it. If it works, it was still your idea. I am less likely to own the win. I will attribute it to you, especially if it was new information to me.

If I come up with an idea and, with your support, implement it, achieving a successful outcome, *I* will own the win. Both my knowledge and confidence grow. I am much stronger from this event than I am from the former.

Telling versus Observing and Asking

If you tell me, I feel "told." You stay the leader, and I stay the follower. Only if you ask in a neutral way, requiring me to think things through, do I grow in my leadership skills. You can make direct observations, but the most powerful mentors support developing leaders to find their own way.

Is it a longer path to immediate results? Yes, it is. Yet, it's the only way people internalize the lessons that are made available to them. With these internalized lessons your people will grow, not just in knowledge. But eventually, wisdom starts to emerge.

This is where leadership development gets exciting, certainly for the mentor.

New perspectives are not the easiest to master. Managers need support from their leaders.

Further, if a leader is consistently using the "Observations and Questions" method of engaging managers and other team leaders in dialogue, the perspective of replacing telling with observations and questions will eventually become part of the manager's natural style of supporting the people on their teams too.

Your people win big from this approach. They are supported by credible, influential managers rather than people who feel the need to exert their prescribed power to get things done.

This is how leaders grow both managers and other leaders for the growth and prosperity of the company, and most of all, the people within.

It's not so bad for business owners who want to gain more freedom either.

14

PREPARE FOR UNEXPECTED CHANGE

NOTHING DERAILS PLANS FOR BUSINESS GROWTH AND PERSONAL freedom faster than unexpected change. Just when you think you're absorbing and dealing with planned changes, an unexpected event can throw everything completely out of whack.

Accounting for Human Behavior: A Series of New Habits

Change can be hard. In this book, I've introduced many new ways of thinking and habits you may need to develop. Shifting how you hire, support, and grow your people takes different skills than the ones you are used to using. These new skills are not yet part of your habitual ways of working.

Habit Development and Unexpected Change

Getting hit with an unexpected change, even a positive change, can interfere with progress and undo habits that have not yet crystalized to become your core ways of operating.

If you're like me, and something unexpected shows up (tell me if there's ever a time in your business when it doesn't), you risk reverting back to what you already know—your old habits. New, developing habits are instinctively set aside while you deal with the new circumstance.

That has huge, unfortunate consequences.

Dealing with changes that occur within your business can be daunting at the best of times. Even with planned changes, areas of fall-out can happen unexpectedly.

New actions will grow into habits over time, but they need that time to develop, mature, and solidify into the core of how you operate your business. Until these are well-entrenched, they may be dislodged with any significant change you encounter.

This applies to everyone in your organization.

Gaining these new ways of operating as well-established norms involves understanding and dealing with human behavior at a whole different level. While eventually rewarding, it does need practice at new ways of thinking and new habit development, which both take time.

People need to acclimatize to new support structures, shifting relationships, new ways of operating with your staff, the promotion and growth of your managers and leaders, or dealing with the impact of marketing and sales campaigns that go much better than expected. Changes, even desirable ones, can be hard.

Unexpected Changes—What Happens?

When changes are unexpected, these shifts will spike your stress levels. Fears over an uncertain future leak into otherwise positive minds. Sometimes they flood in, overtaking thinking completely.

When unexpected changes happen, either within the business, or within the marketplace, owners risk suffering from an "amygdala hijacking." This is when the fear-based emotions take over, throwing everything off course. This is an excellent example of how survival instincts make business roles harder to achieve.

Many, if not all, of the best laid plans get scuttled as you try to sort out the consequences of the changes and how they impact your company.

Predicting Unexpected Changes?

What if you could predict these unexpected changes? Then you could be prepared for them when they show up.

There's only one problem with this thought. You can't predict unexpected changes. By their very nature, unexpected changes are, well, unexpected. That's why we call them that.

Despite this, you want to develop ways to protect the business from any negative consequences. This is like advanced bad-weather warnings. If you know what's coming, we can make plans to deal with it.

The Good News

The good news is that predicting specific changes isn't necessary to protect a business from their impact. What matters is understanding the potential *consequences* of change rather than the changes themselves.

The consequences of changes can be predicted.

> They will leave the business better off, worse off, or roughly the same.

That's the only part you need. Everything else is bonus.

The first type is unexpected but welcome change that has the potential to leave you better off.

1. Changes for the Better

Even positive changes—like major growth opportunities—can create significant challenges for a service business. While these changes ultimately strengthen a company, they require careful navigation to avoid destabilizing the organization.

These opportunities can arise in many forms: a major client suddenly wanting to dramatically increase their business with you, multiple new clients arriving simultaneously due to market shifts, or the chance to expand into new markets or services. While welcome, such rapid growth often reveals that a company isn't fully prepared to handle the increased demand.

Everyone agrees these opportunities are worth pursuing. Yet they bring their own kinds of stress— the pressure to quickly scale up resources, train new people, and maintain quality standards during rapid expansion.

2. The Same, Only Different

A second category of changes may leave your company with no net gain but still require major adjustments. These situations force significant operational shifts or investments just to maintain the status quo.

Common examples include the need to upgrade critical business systems that have become outdated or overwhelmed, having to relocate offices, or dealing with the constant shuffling of project resources when multiple large projects start and stop at unpredictable times. While these changes don't directly improve the bottom line, they cannot be avoided without risking the business's stability.

Even though the long-term result may eventually be positive, the immediate impact feels like running harder just to stay in the same place.

3. Changes that Hurt

The third category of changes are those that leave a business worse off—either temporarily or for an extended period. These unwelcome shifts can come from multiple directions: economic downturns, loss of key staff or clients, regulatory changes, or technological disruptions that make current service offerings less relevant.

The impact can range from a temporary setback lasting six months to two years, to fundamental changes that require completely rethinking how the business operates. While some of these situations resolve naturally with time, others demand active intervention to protect the organization.

These changes test a company's resilience. The businesses that survive and eventually thrive through these periods are invariably those that had prepared for rough times during good ones.

How to Plan for Unexpected Changes

While your crystal ball may be fuzzy on predicting specific unexpected changes, the planning and preparation are far simpler than you may realize.

To properly prepare for these events, you only need two things:

1. Access to additional skilled people, and
2. Sufficient financial reserves.

1. Access to Additional Skilled People

In an expertise-driven company, your people are instrumental in delivering the services. The stronger the demand for staff resources, the higher the need for skilled people.

Building deeper staffing resources than you need for normal operations isn't just prudent. It's essential for handling unexpected change. Most successful firms maintain a buffer of anywhere from 5–15 percent more staff than their current projects require. Since your people need to be highly skilled in order to do their jobs well, you can't assume you can do just-in-time hiring and throw new people at a project. This means moving beyond the traditional approach of hiring just enough people to handle current work.

Three key strategies will help prepare your company:

1. **Maintain a slightly larger team than you currently need**. These people should be actively contributing while providing extra capacity that can be redirected when sudden opportunities or challenges arise.

2. **Develop extensive cross-training throughout your organization**. When people can flex between different roles and projects, your whole operation becomes more adaptable. This isn't just about having backups. It's about growing the capabilities of the entire team.

3. **Build a reliable network of qualified contractors and part-time staff** who understand your business and can step in during transitions. Think of this as your extended bench of talent.

These strategies serve you in all types of change:

- When **positive changes** arrive—like that major growth opportunity you've been hoping for— you'll have pretrained staff ready to step up and trusted contractors who can fill gaps quickly.
- During those **neutral but necessary changes** like system upgrades or project shuffles, your cross-trained team members can temporarily shift their focus while maintaining productivity.
- If you face **negative changes**, this flexibility lets you adjust staffing arrangements while protecting your core operations.

The most resilient companies I've worked with implement these strategies during stable periods. They treat deeper staffing resources as an ongoing investment rather than an emergency response. After all, waiting until you're in the middle of a major change is far too late.

The other major area to prepare, when planning for unexpected change is your financial reserves.

2. Build Sufficient Financial Reserves

Just like with deepening your bench of skilled team members, financial reserves play a vital role in managing all types of unexpected change.

- For **positive changes**, like growth opportunities, reserves provide the working capital needed to bring in more people, invest in training, or expand infrastructure without disrupting existing operations.
- For **neutral changes**, like system upgrades, having extra cash makes these necessary investments less stressful as they don't pull from the day-to-day capital you need to run the business.
- For **negative changes** that impact profits and incoming work, financial reserves can make the difference between weathering a storm comfortably or struggling to survive.

Building these reserves takes time and discipline. The most successful companies I work with commit to setting aside a percentage of revenue consistently, treating it like any other critical business expense. While the exact amount varies by company and industry, the key is making it a regular habit rather than waiting for occasional windfalls.

Here's an example of how this works. I recently reconnected with a business owner who discovered a potential four-hundred-thousand-dollar liability that could hit within two to three years. Rather than panic, he developed a plan to set aside 5 percent of gross revenue while also securing a larger line of credit. This combination of active saving and expanded credit access turned a serious threat into a manageable challenge.

The most remarkable outcome wasn't just the financial security. It was how this preparation affected the whole organization. Once the owner had a clear plan for building reserves, his anxiety decreased noticeably. His team reported he regained his entrepreneurial spark, and opportunities that previously seemed daunting became exciting possibilities again.

This highlights a crucial truth. Financial reserves don't just protect your business. They provide the confidence to pursue growth and handle whatever changes arise along the way.

Increasing Freedom

With a deeper bench of talent available to you, and with sufficient financial reserves at your fingertips, you will naturally expand your freedoms, both **in** your business and **from** it as well. This also improves your ability to grow the third freedom, the larger asset value you are generating, multiplying your reach and impact, or whatever other commitments are driving you. You are effectively increasing your freedom **because of** this business of yours.

Exciting stuff!

15

THE FREEDOM FRAMEWORK

YOUR ESTABLISHED, EXPERTISE-DRIVEN SERVICES COMPANY HAS many moving parts. When you opened shop or bought into this company, you thought the growth of the expertise was the biggest requirement to make it work.

And you were right.

Without growing expertise, you will be left behind in your marketplace. Or you could be relegated to a price-driven pit of commodity-based competition. That's no fun at all.

That also doesn't give you any increased freedom.

Through these chapters we have walked through the components of how to build an intelligent ecosystem. If done well, you'll enjoy endless opportunities for gaining the freedom you seek.

The Freedom Framework

This framework includes seven essential elements.

1. Rethink the Core

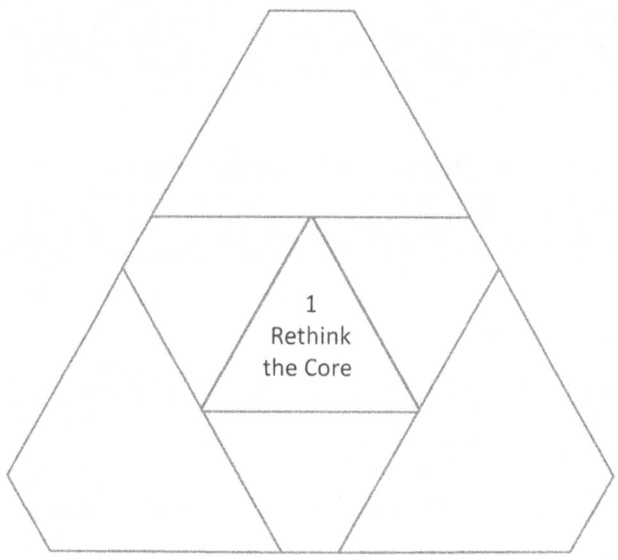

Figure 15.1

While many actions shift, this first piece of the framework is more a series of three new perspectives to take rather than actions to implement. The actions follow in the subsequent elements.

The first new perspective is to consider your people as a fundamental part of your business's core, rather than mechanistic inputs to it. If they are not truly treated as part of the core, the development of an ecosystem that grants you more freedom will, simply put, risk failure.

All the remaining pieces of this puzzle rely on this one foundational perspective as you work on the growth of your business.

The second perspective shift is to understand how fundamental human behavior affects the inner workings of your business. By recognizing how four key behavioral drivers shape actions and reactions, you gain invaluable insights into what motivates your team members.

These are:

1. Survival—acting to protect ourselves in the face of threats
2. Thriving—seeking opportunities to grow and advance
3. Connection—working together so the environment feels safe and rewarding
4. Adaptation—adjusting to meet changing circumstances

The third perspective is to realize that modern expectations have fundamentally shifted. Technology and generational shifts have created new workplace expectations. How you operate and grow your business must change to meet these expectations.

The core perspective shifts give you access to increase your freedom at three levels.

What are the actions to take, and the habits to develop, to build, maintain, and grow an intelligent ecosystem that will increase your access to freedom?

That's where the rest of the framework comes in.

2. Hire Smart

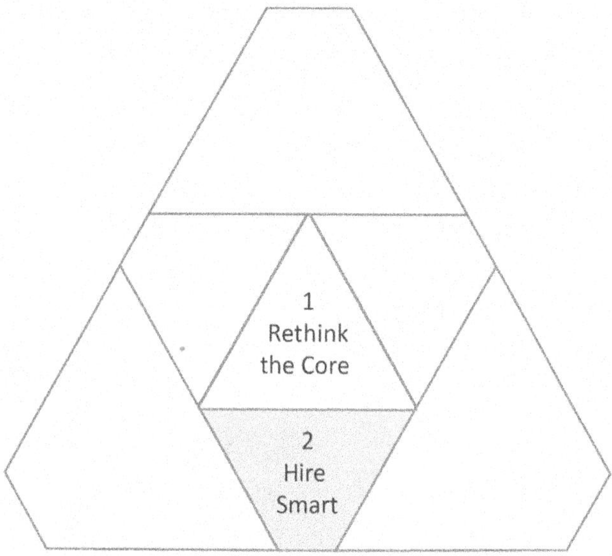

Figure 15.2

Hiring the right-fit people requires new ways of conducting searches while learning to rely on different perspectives than you may have previously used (as detailed in chapter 9).

The biggest shift is to only consider people who could become potential partners or close allies in your company. This doesn't mean only hiring high-priced help. It's about mind-set. There is a fundamental difference between people who focus on themselves versus those who naturally focus on making a difference for others. At all levels, you want to find the second type of person. This is more a function of mind-set than career stage. You'll find both types of people across all age groups and experience levels.

The Social Contract we explored in chapter 8 becomes your foundation for both hiring new staff and working with your existing people. It keeps your focus on professional growth, helping you bring people in with professional growth as a key priority.

While transforming your organization's hiring practices may take one to two years—longer for larger companies—you'll see the positive impact of these improvements quickly. Each right-fit person you bring on board directly increases your levels of freedom.

3. Train and Grow People

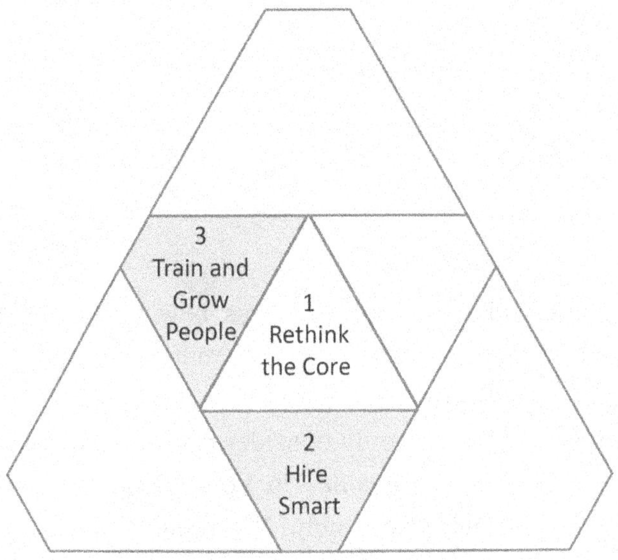

Figure 15.3

With the Social Contract (chapter 8) as your foundation and your people as key to your company's core (chapter 7), supporting professional growth becomes essential. However, this requires more than good intentions. It means actively integrating development into your already-full schedule.

Training and growing your people is not merely an add-on

activity. As explored in chapter 10, it's fundamental to building your ecosystem. This requires implementing structured approaches like job roles and growth plans for each team member. Integrating these two items serves your employees by making their progress front and center, while saving you and your managers time, by dealing with the job role and people's growth concurrently.

This may be the hardest shift to integrate into your daily activities, but it also offers the highest potential return. By investing in your people's development, you simultaneously strengthen your company's capabilities and increase your own freedom. The results impact both the operation and growth of your business while accelerating your path to the freedom you seek.

4. Focus on Teams

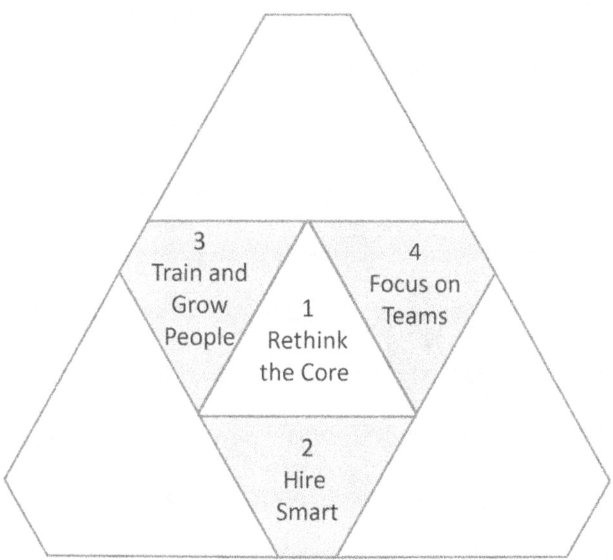

Figure 15.4

Teamwork allows your firm to deliver collective results that are larger than any one person could produce (as explored in chapter 11). Whether in groups of two people or ten, teamwork is essential.

Your company's experts and specialists have naturally developed and reinforced strong habits that support effective individual project delivery. However, many of those habits need to be refined to support collaborative work in teams.

Your work with teams also impacts how you choose the structures for growth. You can measure progress using various models—whether a hybrid team with homeroom structure, a mentoring system, or other approaches that directly support people's growth. The key is maintaining focus on client value while developing your team's collaborative capabilities.

This focus ensures the strength and sustainability of your organization more than any other.

5. Grow Managers

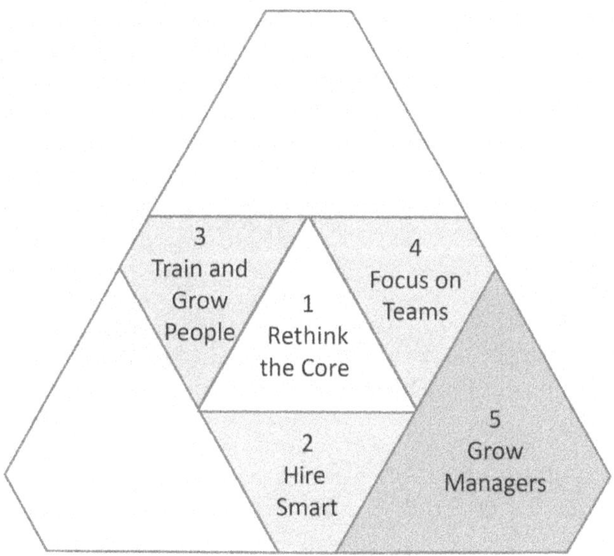

Figure 15.5

As explored in chapter 12, managers need to expand their focus to include not only setting and delivering project goals but also individual staff goals for professional growth and team development. These require new habits and approaches.

The transition to management requires a fundamental shift in how people use their expertise. While technical excellence may have earned them the promotion, success as a manager requires moving from prescribed power based on expertise to earned influence based on credibility. This means learning to train, support, coordinate, and facilitate results while allowing their team members' best thinking to emerge.

Building and developing trust-based relationships becomes the focus of their new role. Managers must learn how to grow an intelligent ecosystem and develop habits to support this more productive focus.

6. Develop Leaders

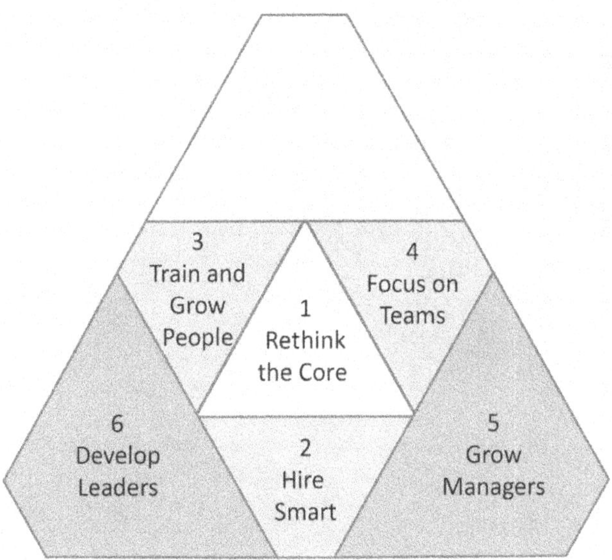

Figure 15.6

Leaders supporting managers in their role through mentoring and guidance—rather than dictating instructions—once again requires new habits to be established and developed. As explored in chapter 13, the goal is to help managers "rally people to a brighter future."

This means teaching leaders how to expand beyond traditional management functions to fulfill four critical roles:

- Creating and unfolding a compelling future
- Standing for and actively strengthening the corporate culture
- Supporting managers in developing their teams and team members
- Developing and growing existing and future leaders within the company

Developing leadership skills in managers means shifting from telling and directing to using observations and questions that provoke independent thought. Leaders must learn to support their managers in seeing situations from a higher altitude and longer view while showing genuine care for people's growth and prosperity. Most importantly, they need to trust in their teams' ability to figure things out, providing guidance rather than control.

7. Prepare for Unexpected Change

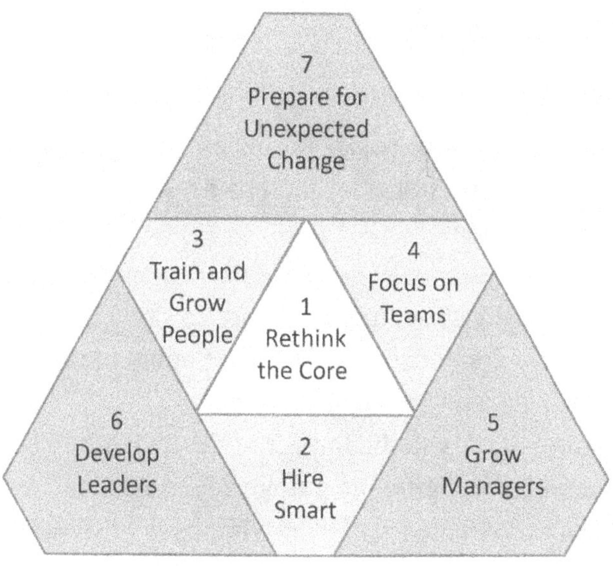

Figure 15.7

Planning and preparation for what could catch you off guard, as discussed in chapter 14, means being ready for three types of situations: welcomed opportunities, necessary transitions, and challenging setbacks. Success in any of these scenarios requires two key elements: skilled people and financial reserves.

Actively look to bolster your bench strength, whether through expanding your network of reliable outside contractors or cross-training your existing team. This may also include keeping slightly higher staffing levels. This provides the wiggle room to immediately embrace opportunities when they arise.

Equally important is methodically growing your financial reserves. This provides the peace of mind and freedom to take steps that might otherwise feel scary.

Collectively, these seven parts come together to provide the key elements of an intelligent ecosystem, inside which your people may flourish, grow the company, and grow in their own respective ways.

This creates the freedom you're after in your business.

The Danger Zones

The danger zones, those pesky obstacles lurking beneath each of the major growth milestones of the business, are formed from two fundamental dynamics:

1. Outstripping structures and processes that served the company previously but no longer apply at its new larger size, combined with
2. A misread of both the impact of the lack of revised structures on a growing employee base and an attempt to control people's behavior with the new structures, rather than implementing systems and processes to make it easier for people to bring their best.

If the perspectives identified in The Freedom Framework are applied consistently, they have a series of positive influences on the business as it continues to grow.

But what about the structures themselves? How does this new framework apply to each danger zone? What structures need to be shifted and how?

Let's take a look at a few of the structures you face at each milestone of growth.

A Fundamental Perspective

Each of the elements of The Freedom Framework apply to all the danger zones. Paramount to this is the notion that an expertise-driven service business needs to be developed as an intelligent ecosystem. Once mastered, this core premise, and what follows from it, provides access to the increased freedom you seek.

Structures for Danger Zone 1—Approaching Revenue of Two (or Three) Million Dollars

To build the company up to and past its first million in revenue, people who came into the company needed the flexibility to adapt to varying situations. As a result, you probably hired what we call "utility players." People who could operate relatively well in any number of roles were preferred to specialists. After that first million, however, this changes. Hiring needs to be more focused on intermediate and senior people (or juniors with specific skills) who may grow in their specialties over time. The individual growth plans of your people will help you uncover any hidden aspirations that may exist.

When seeking a budding manager or team leader to promote from within the company's ranks, instead of looking at the most effective practitioner to lead the others, you might want to identify who is effective in supporting others on the team to learn and grow.

If no one is skilled in this area, you will be on the lookout, as you grow toward two million in revenue, for someone who includes these attributes.[1]

Structures for Danger Zone 2—The Other Side of Five Million

As the company approaches and moves beyond five million dollars, you will feel the impact of the additional staff at these stronger levels. As you outstrip your structures, the focus needs to be squarely on what would support people to be at their best rather than what structures will get people to do what you want.

Really easy to say, but much harder to achieve.

Of course, with rigor in hiring—only taking on potential partners and close allies to your teams—many of these issues dissipate.

Increased training on teamwork starts to have a larger impact at and after five million in revenue, as you build higher number of teams in the company. If this is combined with connection points among managers, where they may share their experiences and ideas with each other, siloes that might otherwise creep in never have the chance to do so.

When people are connected with each other, whether team members or managers with fellow managers, progress accelerates and things get easier for everyone.

Your growing leaders start to make a real impact on the organization's effectiveness at this point.

If you haven't already had the chance, now is the time to start building your financial reserves and the depth of your access to other experts who might join your team as you grow. This foresight

1. For the list of ten attributes of an effective manager, please go to FreedomBookResources.com.

will pay dividends every step of the way, decreasing your stress and increasing your freedom in the process.

Structures for Danger Zone 3—Approaching Ten Million

As a company heads toward ten million in revenue, the numbers of people and managers have been expanding. Training and growing people, while keeping a results focus, is critical by this point.

Team training and development along with the support of the growth of managers all play an integral role in allowing you to support your people to bring their best. After all, since you are hiring the best-fit people for your organization, professional growth and opportunities to contribute in meaningful ways are exactly what they crave, even as they grow in their profession or trade.

Between five million and ten million dollars is where the need for effective leaders becomes obvious. As you approach ten million, any shortfall in the leadership team reverberates through the company. Treating this area of the company as a key priority makes life better for everyone. The more actively your leaders can support the growth of your managers and team leads, the more positive and productive life will be within your walls.

Growth plans play an integral role throughout the growth of the company. By the time the company is at this level, the impact will have compounded. The freedom is real.

Haven't added this piece yet? No problem. Now is a great time to start or continue to weave together this intellectual ecosystem using this, one of the most powerful tools available from this book. The quiet, yet far-reaching, impact of individual career development plans (growth plans) for all your people, integrated with each person's job role, cannot be overstated.

Structures for Danger Zone 4—The Chasm Between Twelve Million and Twenty Million Dollars

At this point, your business is too big for the current infrastructure yet too small to maximize the returns for an expanded series of needed systems.

This becomes an ideal time to rethink the whole business.

You can stop at ten to twelve million in revenue, or you can invest and get to twenty million as quickly as possible, hopefully within two years. Somewhere between eighteen and twenty million dollars, the profits start to spring back as if they never left.

It goes easier and faster, limited only by your ability to attract the right-fit staff for each part of your company, if you adopt the challenge to develop your intelligent ecosystem as a fundamental key to your organization's make-up.

The Freedom Framework, combined with constant proactive assessments of your structures as instruments to support your people in their individual and collective commitments to bring their best, will give you access to the brighter future you seek.

More on that next.

16

CREATE A BRIGHTER FUTURE

GROWING AN EXPERTISE-BASED BUSINESS CAN FEEL overwhelming. Every day brings new challenges— from finding and retaining great people to maintaining quality as you scale, preserving your own energy and enthusiasm through it all. The constant juggling of competing priorities can make your dream of freedom feel like it's never going to happen.

Yet these very challenges provide the path forward. What all businesses have in common, especially those driven by the expertise and skills of their people, is the need to address the underlying dynamics present when people work with each other. While this human element can make growth more complex, it also holds the key to unlocking greater freedom and success.

Every business grows a little differently. The reason is simple. Every business has different people within it, with their own strengths, ambitions, and ideas. If you were not able to tap the power of the human element, your business would suffer, and so would you.

In fact, not everyone taps the power of their people, and they do suffer. These companies get stuck in the danger zones we discussed—struggling with senior support at two million in revenue, cycling between five million and seven million with quality issues and declining profits, hitting walls approaching ten million due to inconsistent team performance, or getting trapped in that chasm between twelve million and twenty million dollars where margins erode and politics take over. They cycle in place, watching their best people leave while wondering why their proven expertise isn't enough anymore.

The framework we covered in the second half of this book shows a different path. By rethinking the core of your business to include your people, hiring for partnership potential, and focusing on professional growth, you create the foundation for sustainable success. When you add effective teams, strong managers, and developing leaders, you build an ecosystem that can weather unexpected changes.

There really are as many ways to grow a business as there are people. There are also as many ways to overcome similar challenges as there are people. After all, we each have something unique to bring to the table.

To grow a business takes a lot. The existence of your people can make it harder but only if you try to control rather than support them.

Yet if you implement the framework we discussed—if you learn what makes your people tick and support their growth—the journey becomes much easier. Your teams begin collaborating naturally. Your managers focus on developing people rather than just directing them. Your leaders create the environment where everyone can thrive.

Oh, yes, you will have your work cut out for you, but your people, with all their quirks, idiosyncrasies, and behavioral wiring, are also the source of your business power.

Every business problem you run into as you grow your company may be solved by making your people your top priority

—not just in words but through the specific actions we've discussed. When you build proper support structures, implement effective growth plans, and create the right environment, amazing results follow.

An ecosystem may appear daunting, but by implementing each piece of the framework systematically—from hiring through leadership development—while preparing for unexpected change, you can get there.

Now that you are armed with additional information about the impact of human behavior on your business growth, you will be able to grow your company more smoothly in service of your clients and customers, your internal teams, your family, and your community.

Everything comes back to one simple notion. By making your people your top priority, life goes better.

The ingredients we covered in these pages will give you the freedom you desire.

Those freedoms are:

1. **Your freedom *in* your business** to do work that lights you up and allows you to grow as an owner and a professional, while your capable teams handle the rest.
2. **Your freedom *from* your business**, to take time away and enjoy the many other parts of life that are available to us all, knowing your well-trained managers and leaders will maintain quality and keep projects moving forward.
3. **The freedom *because of* your business**, to reap the financial rewards of a smoothly running operation and to see your impact multiply through the growth of your people.

As you work in the areas that you find most satisfying, you will find your business to be more enjoyable. The relationships within your company will deepen as trust builds through your investment in people's growth. You'll find yourself taking more time off, truly unplugged, as your ecosystem functions effectively without constant oversight.

When you come back, you will find yourself fresher since the main sources of anxiety are well in hand.

Most importantly, you will find that you have regained the excitement you had when you started on this journey. Only now, that excitement comes from seeing your whole organization thrive, not just from your individual expertise.

Seeking your own freedom may seem like a selfish act. However, I hope you have come to realize that in striving for increased freedom, you set up your organization to flourish, not only for yourself but for the others in this ecosystem you have built.

Together, we are stronger.

DO YOU WANT TO GROW YOUR BUSINESS?

Are you ready to take your business to the next level?

For over 30 years, we have supported business owners of all sizes to take their business to the next level. If you would like to explore possibilities, either drop us a line or give us a call.

Join our business community of like-minded business owners - useful articles and constructive dialogues.

info@walshbusinessgrowth.com

Ph: (604) 263-5670

Or check out our web-site: www.walshbusinessgrowth.com
Serving business owners in Canada, USA, UK, and Europe.

Remember: Together we are stronger.

ACKNOWLEDGMENTS

There are usually only one or two names that adorn most books as author. That has very little to do with how many people it takes to create a book. Both with myself, and with most people I know, there are many people involved in the creation of the ideas within this book, as well as their practical implementation.

I have learned so much from clients as we have worked together in support of not only their goals and dreams, but also digging in to move past the issues and stumbling blocks that got in their way, through their journey.

The larger business community shares ideas at conferences and in the many books, articles, and debates on what makes a difference in the life of business owners, new and established alike. Steve Alper worked with me to help me clarify my thinking (no easy task) in early versions of this effort. Many thanks, Steve.

I was privileged to work with and learn from Tim Grahl, CEO of StoryGrid, who agreed to be my developmental editor for this project. He both steered my writing and was invaluable in moving this whole process forward. Tim, I am forever in your debt.

Ying Lin has been instrumental in developing all the diagrams and many logistics in pulling this effort together. Thanks, Ying!

Lauren Reid is a social media star. She has guided me through my LinkedIn learning curve. She continues to stretch me to grow in this previously unknown domain of business.

To the advanced readers who gave me incredible feedback, I couldn't have made this half as strong without your input. Special thanks to Mike Nott and to Kim Morrow for your detailed reviews and words of encouragement! Much appreciated!

Thank you, Kim Folsom, for your contribution in writing the Foreword to this book. The work you do in helping USA business owners to gain access to funding for their growth is truly admirable.

Carlyn Craig of Post Hypnotic Press has been a treat to work with in creating the audible version of this book. You have my appreciation. No wonder everyone says you are the best audible resource!

Govindh Jayaraman, I enjoyed working with you on your Paper Napkin Wisdom podcasts. Thanks for the opportunity to dig in while sharing the notions contained in this book. I appreciate the opportunity to work with you again!

The person who deserves the most credit is Grace, who encouraged me during the frustrating times and put up with me way more than I deserve. You have my heart.

Michael

ABOUT THE AUTHOR

Michael Walsh is a visionary leader, speaker, and author known for igniting passion in the business owners and senior leaders he works with by helping them to drive their established businesses to growth levels beyond their expectations.

In this, his third book, he gives people direct access to increased freedom using 21st century strategies that work.

For over 30 years, as founder and President of Walsh Business Growth Institute, Michael has supported business owners to grow their businesses in service of their goals and commitments in life.

He also lives what he teaches. Applying his methods, he has built his company to take eighteen weeks off each year for personal travel, together with his family.

www.ingramcontent.com/pod-product-compliance
Lightning Source LLC
Chambersburg PA
CBHW071550200326
41519CB00021BB/6690

9780995333024